CHILD CUSTODY & DOMESTIC VIOLENCE

To Deb for her love, patience, and help
in finding some balance in my life. P. J.

To my friend Harriette Davis,
her three children, and her seven grandchildren,
who continue on a daily basis to be impacted
by the justice system's failure to assist her
in escaping an abusive relationship
almost 20 years ago. N. L.

To the matriarchs in my life
who showed me the many faces of courage:
my mother Shirley, my grandmother Libby,
and my guardian Ann. You are missed always. S. P.

CHILD CUSTODY & DOMESTIC VIOLENCE

A Call for Safety and Accountability

Peter G. Jaffe
The Centre for Children & Families in the Justice System

Nancy K. D. Lemon
University of California, Berkeley

Samantha E. Poisson
The Centre for Children & Families in the Justice System

SAGE Publications
International Educational and Professional Publisher
Thousand Oaks ▪ London ▪ New Delhi

For information:

Sage Publications, Inc.
2455 Teller Road
Thousand Oaks, California 91320
E-mail: order@sagepub.com

Sage Publications Ltd.
6 Bonhill Street
London EC2A 4PU
United Kingdom

Sage Publications India Pvt. Ltd.
M-32 Market
Greater Kailash I
New Delhi 110 048 India

Printed in the United States of America

Library of Congress Cataloging-in-Publication Data

Jaffe, Peter G.
Child custody and domestic violence: A call for safety and accountability / Peter G. Jaffe, Nancy K. D. Lemon, Samantha E. Poisson.
p. cm.
Includes bibliographical references and index.
ISBN 0-7619-1825-6 (c)— ISBN 0-7619-1826-4 (p) 1. Custody of children—Law and legislation. 2. Family violence—Law and legislation. 3. Child witnesses. 4. Parental alienation syndrome. I. Lemon, Nancy K. D., 1953- II. Poisson, Samantha E. III. Title.
K707 .J34 2003
346.01'73—dc21
2002010311

This book is printed on acid-free paper.

06 07 08 09 10 10 9 8 7 6 5 4 3

Acquisitions Editor:	Margaret H. Seawell
Editorial Assistant:	Alicia Carter
Production Editor:	Olivia Weber
Copy Editor:	Annette R. Pagliaro
Typesetter:	Bramble Books
Indexer:	Teri Greenberg
Cover Designer:	Sandra Ng

Contents

Preface

There has been tremendous progress in the public and professional understanding of the plight of children caught in the middle of custody disputes. The stigma attached to divorce in the past has dissipated; today, divorce and separation are understood to be painful crises in the lives of children and adults. Rather than being outcasts, children and parents have access to a host of services to counsel them through their ordeal. Friends, relatives, and colleagues at work may offer the names of helpful lawyers to resolve the dispute. Parent-education programs are available to assist parents in finding cost-effective solutions to their conflicts, and most jurisdictions in North America have mediation services.

As the findings of major research studies on children of divorce have become common knowledge (Hetherington & Kelly, 2002; Wallerstein, Lewis, & Blakeslee, 2000), social attitudes toward divorce have changed. The issue has received widespread media attention, with publications such as *Time* magazine devoting cover stories to children of divorce (Kirn, 2000). Although it is recognized that children may be adversely affected by divorce, there is general agreement that children's adjustment improves when postseparation conflict ends and their relationship with both parents is supported and sustained. In other words, divorce ends marital relationships, not parent–child relationships.

Today, fathers play a more active role in parenting and nurturing their children than they likely experienced with their own fathers. Both parents offer their children love, education, support, and guidance through the most critical phases of development. At the dawn of a new millennium, society and the courts often look to mothers and fathers as partners in raising their children, both before and after separation. Parental involvement is no longer intractably wed to gender.

In dealing with separation and divorce, legal and mental health professionals assist in the development of parenting plans in which both parents play an active and meaningful role. Messages of "coparenting" and "shared parenting" are promoted and viewed as very much in keeping with the best interests of children post-separation. Several research studies have found that children adjust better in joint custody postseparation arrangements than in sole custody arrangements. Although there is an obvious bias in this research because less conflictual divorces make for better adjusted parents and children at the outset, there is a general agreement among the public and professionals that cooperation and coparenting is much better than litigation and postdivorce acrimony. The popular press has even promoted "happy" divorces for which parents can find lawyers who will "collaborate" rather than litigate (Underwood, 2002).

Over the past 25 years, many families have benefited from court reforms and legislative changes promoting joint custody and shared parenting arrangements. This progress has come with a genuine desire to improve the quality of children's postdivorce experience. At the same time, there remains considerable debate on the accessibility and effectiveness of various forms of legal and clinical remedies and interventions. New controversies and challenges have emerged around such issues as parental mobility (Irving & Benjamin, 1996), grandparent rights (Shaffer, 2001), and the increasing rate of same-sex parent separation (Hartman, 1996). Few issues, however, have sparked more passionate public discussion than custody disputes involving allegations of domestic violence.

This book focuses on the complexity of this issue and the challenges facing judges, lawyers, legislators, and mental health professionals in developing safe and effective response strategies. Most separating parents are able to resolve their disputes over custody and visitation with minimal intervention from the legal and mental health systems (Johnston, 1994). As authors, we endorse the active and meaningful postseparation involvement of both parents with their children, in the absence of a history of domestic violence. However, the presence of domestic violence within a custody dispute demands a different analysis and distinct interventions by judges, policymakers, and mental health professionals.

This book is neither for nor against mothers or fathers. It is directed to the safety and security of separating parents and children in circumstances of domestic violence. Its intended audience is legal and mental health professionals who provide services to divorcing parents and who should be alerted to the unique dynamics and aftermath of domestic violence. This book may also be helpful to those who have found their lives and their children's lives affected by domestic violence, and can assist close friends and relatives providing support for victims of domestic violence to broaden their understanding of the issues.

Chapter 1 provides an overview of the terrain, including the prevalence of divorce and domestic violence, the relevance of domestic violence in custody disputes, and the intensity of the debate surrounding this subject. Chapter 2 focuses on the evaluation of the meaning of domestic violence allegations in custody disputes for mothers, fathers, and children. Special effort is made to assist those attempting to determine whether a history of violence exists within a family. The chapter also addresses such thorny issues as parent alienation syndrome, false allegations, and mutual abuse. Chapter 3 reviews the relevant legislation and guidelines applicable to custody disputes involving domestic violence in four countries: the United States, Canada, New Zealand, and Australia. Chapter 4 outlines significant judicial decisions in these four countries, the scope of which highlights the inconsistency and unpredictability of recent judgements and reveals how well-intended legislation does not always produce the desired outcome. Chapter 5 ends the book with recommendations for legislative improvements, increased training for legal and mental health professionals, enhanced services and programs, and the development of new policies to deal with domestic violence in custody disputes.

Acknowledgments

Although this book took 4 years from inception to publication, the time delays were well spent. The legal and mental health concerns of our clients invariably took precedence over precious writing time. The positive by-product of the delay is that it gave us countless additional hours to do research and ground our thoughts in the clinical feedback from our clients around the challenges they face in the court system, as well as the dilemmas posed by professionals in our training sessions. The three of us benefited from several conferences on children exposed to domestic violence where we role-played in mock trial situations the many difficult issues that judges, lawyers, and custody evaluators face on a daily basis. Through our countless e-mails and phone conversations we believe we have been able to produce a valuable resource that can be digested readily by individuals representing a variety of disciplines and viewpoints, including frontline advocates and parents trying to make sense of their courtroom situations.

For two of us (P. J. & S. P.), working at the Centre for Children & Families in the Justice System, this book would not have been possible without the support of the Atkinson Foundation, who funded a 3-year research project examining the plight of abused women and children seeking refuge from batterers and safety in the court system. The voices of women and children from this research, as well as our clinical work, form the foundation for many of the ideas outlined in this book. This book would not have been completed without the encouragement of staff and board members at our Centre. In particular, we received adept assistance from Andrea Finlay in helping with the literature review and organizing hundreds of references; Karen Chalmers provided expert clerical support in the many revisions of the document and broad shoulders in times of setback; and Peggy Sattler provided invaluable assistance in editing our original manuscript for greater clarity.

We continue to receive phone calls and e-mails from abused women across North America who are desperately seeking our help in having a custody evaluator, lawyer, or judge understand their unique circumstances in the aftermath of domestic violence. The experiences of these women have been echoed in many jurisdictions around the world. It is always striking that when the three of us discuss the plight of abused women and children it seems almost irrelevant whether one of us is in London, Ontario, or Berkeley, California. Domestic violence and revictimization through the court system knows no jurisdictional boundaries. We wrote this book for abused women, their children, and the multiple professionals they come into contact with in the court system.

For all the abused women who continue to call and e-mail us, seeking help with complex and lengthy custody battles in a confusing, expensive, and often biased legal system, we wish we could give each one of you the help you and your children truly need. We hope this book will help prevent some of the stories you have told us from happening to more mothers and children.

1

Why Domestic Violence Is Relevant in Child-Custody Disputes

Everyone is touched by divorce. Separating parents turn to friends, relatives, and colleagues at work for advice and assistance with their new life circumstances. Some parents seek advice in advance, and plan for the pending transition in their lives. Other parents find themselves in unexpected crisis situations and their children in turmoil. Support comes from informal groups, and professionals in the mental health and legal arenas. The challenges in giving meaningful and helpful advice are enormous. Questions such as the following are raised: How will my children be affected by my divorce? What schedule will best meet their needs at various ages? Can I successfully share parenting and decision making with my ex-partner? What role will future stepparents play in my children's lives? The complexity of these questions is underlined by the fact that separation is a process and the impact for all involved is unique and dynamic. In this chapter, we address the issues that all divorcing families face, and then highlight the distinctive plight of children dealing with both separation and domestic violence.

❖ CHILDREN OF DIVORCE

Millions of children across North America have experienced the pain, confusion, and grief that result from divorce. In 1998 alone, 1,135,000 divorces occurred in the United States, representing a rate of 4.2 per 1,000 people (National Center for Health Statistics, 1998). In Canada, a total of 69,088 couples divorced in 1998, which represents a relatively lower rate of 2.2 divorces per 1,000 people (Statistics Canada, 2000b). Based on the Canadian divorce rate, 36% of marriages are expected to end in divorce within 30 years of marriage. Of the approximately 70,000 Canadian couples who divorced in 1998, 21,448 cases involved a custody order for dependent children, representing nearly a third of all divorces in that year. Given the trends with respect to common-law relationships, same-sex relationships, and remarriages, it is probable that these statistics seriously underestimate the number of children coping with the breakdown of their family.

Research on children's postseparation adjustment has painted a confusing and sometimes contradictory portrait of how children are affected by divorce and postseparation contact with each parent. As a result of these mixed messages, policymakers, legislators, and the community at large have drawn sweeping conclusions about all divorcing families with little or no awareness of the differences between families. Some researchers have found that divorce per se is highly traumatizing and can create a lifelong legacy of relationship problems, low self-esteem, and lowered social competency. Other research studies have concluded that a child experiencing divorce may be relatively unscathed. It may be that researchers' failure to clearly define and consider the nature of the interpersonal conflict both prior to and following marital dissolution has resulted in such disparate findings. This research deficiency has led the general population, politicians, mental health professionals, policymakers, and judges to base strong, and sometimes unyielding, views about divorce and custody disputes on findings that fail to adequately address the multiplicity of factors affecting children's postseparation adjustment.

In a 12-year longitudinal study involving 471 adult children, Paul Amato and his colleagues (Amato, Loomis, & Booth, 1995) found that the consequences of divorce for children was dependent on the parental conflict prior to divorce. They reported that in high-conflict families, children had higher levels of well-being as young adults if their parents divorced than if they had stayed together. However, in low-conflict families the opposite was the case: Children had higher levels of well-being if their parents stayed together than if they divorced. This type of research moves us toward a more complete understanding of the complexity of the issues, and validates opinions that seem diametrically opposed. Divorce may be harmful for children from some families in certain circumstances, whereas it may be beneficial for children from other families. When divorce is inevitable, the effect on children is partially dependent on the parents' ability to resolve conflicts.

Because resolving child-custody disputes requires separating parents to focus on the needs of the child rather than past hostilities and adult grievances, disputes are more readily settled when the separation has not harmed the basic trust and respect that is the foundation of parenting. Some disputes may require external interventions such as mediation or consultation with family law lawyers; these interventions require that the parents feel safe and comfortable engaging with one another. With a history of domestic violence, however, professionals cannot instruct or advise parents simply to put the past behind them. These situations require a careful evaluation of the violence, including the possibility that one parent may pose a significant risk to the other parent and the children. It is unreasonable to expect a parent who has experienced physical, sexual, and/or psychological abuse at the hands of the other parent to negotiate custody and visitation agreements when fear is the overriding emotion. Yet because many legal and mental health professionals prize reaching a resolution to the dispute, they may overlook subtle signs that a custody agreement was not reached voluntarily. And in a family court system that reinforces "friendly parents" and is punitive or troubled by the prospect of "difficult parents" raising allegations of abuse, parents who have suffered the violence often feel coerced into settlements that further endanger themselves and their children.

❖ WHAT IS CUSTODY?

Many separating parents do not fully understand what is meant by the term "custody." Custody of a child includes both a legal and physical aspect. Physical custody is the right to physically have the child live with a parent and have visitation (or access) with the other parent.

Legal custody is the right to make major decisions about a child's care, such as a child's education, medical care, and religious upbringing. Physical and legal custody can be sole (the right of only one individual) or joint (a right shared between two or more individuals). In a sole physical custody situation, the child resides primarily with one parent and has visitation with the other. When sole legal custody is in place, one parent has the right to independently make the major decisions affecting the child. Joint physical custody means that the child lives with both parents and joint legal custody means that the parents share the right to make major decisions about the child's care.

❖ DOMESTIC VIOLENCE

Domestic violence is best understood as one intimate partner's attempt to control, dominate, and humiliate the other partner through a variety of means, including physical, sexual, psychological, financial, and spiritual abuse. Domestic violence goes beyond individual acts of aggression to encompass an overall pattern of behavior aimed at maintaining complete control. Researchers and practitioners alike recognize that domestic violence typically escalates in both frequency and severity over time. Without intervention, battering may grow into a habitual method of resolving conflict.

As a field of academic study, the issue of domestic violence is only a quarter century old and most of the advances in the research have occurred recently. In 1980, there were several books and a handful of journal articles featuring domestic violence. Today there are whole sections in major bookstores, many journal articles, and countless Web sites dedicated in large part to the issue of domestic violence.

The statistics reveal a problem much more prevalent than the average citizen would predict. When Murray Straus and his colleagues (1980) completed their initial research for the book *Behind Closed Doors: Violence in American Families,* they were the first social scientists to confirm what the women's movement and battered women's shelter advocates had been saying for some time: Home was not a safe place (Straus, Gelles, & Steinmetz, 1980). Their pioneering research unearthed the reality that millions of men, women, and children lived with violence as an integral part of family life. According to their research, approximately 1 out of 10 women had experienced violence at the hands of the one they loved. Three percent endured severe violence including life-threatening attacks and injuries requiring medical attention.

Many other researchers have confirmed and expanded these findings using a variety of methodologies including phone surveys, police reports, and structured interviews in a range of clinical and community settings. In 1984, the U.S. attorney general declared domestic violence a major social problem that, if tolerated, allows the seeds of violence to be sown in the next generation (Department of the Attorney General, 1984). In 1992, the American Medical Association reported that women were four times more likely to be injured in their homes by their current or former partner than in motor vehicle accidents (American Medical Association, 1992).

A 1993 national study in Canada involving telephone interviews with over 12,000 randomly chosen women found that 29% experienced physical or sexual abuse by an intimate partner over their lifetime (Rodgers, 1994). The definition of abuse used in this study was consistent with the Criminal Code of Canada: The abuse could have resulted in criminal charges with reasonable and probable grounds that it had taken place. Ten percent of women stated that the abuse made them so fearful for their personal safety that they feared for their lives.

In the U.S. National Violence Against Women Survey (Tjaden & Thoennes, 2000), 22.1% of the women and 7.4% of the men surveyed reported they were physically assaulted by a current or former spouse in their lifetime. An estimated 1.3 million women and 835,000 men are physically assaulted by an intimate partner annually in the United States. Further, women are significantly more likely than men to be injured during an assault and the risk of injury increases for women when their assailant is a current or former intimate partner. Approximately one third of injured women receive medical treatment for their injuries.

Statistics from Australia confirm a similarly high rate of domestic violence. According to the Australian Bureau of Statistics, 23% of women experienced violence by a current or former intimate partner in their lifetime (Putt & Higgins, 1997). Although the majority of women indicated that the abuse occurred in a past relationship, 12% of women reported that they lived in fear of abuse during their current relationship. Some groups of women appear especially vulnerable to abuse. For example, in Western Australia, Aboriginal women make up only

3% of the adult female population, but account for half the domestic violence incidents reported to police. The incidents of domestic violence in New Zealand are comparable to those in Australia.

Men can also be victims of domestic violence. In a 2000 study conducted by the Canadian Centre for Justice Statistics, which involved 9,178 women and 7,827 men, the 5-year and 1-year rates of spousal victimization were only slightly higher for women than men (Canadian Centre for Justice Statistics, 2000). Seven percent of men and 8% of women reported being physically assaulted by a current or former partner in the past 5 years. These findings suggest that an estimated 690,000 women and 549,000 men were victims of some form of spousal assault during a 5-year period in Canada.

While data on the prevalence of violence is important, it can camouflage important differences with respect to the nature, severity, and consequences of the violence (Johnson & Bunge, 2001). Statistics such as "7% of men" and "8% of women" have experienced violence at the hands of their partner give rise to the conclusion that women are equally as violent as men. However, a closer examination shows that the violence inflicted and endured is qualitatively different. Women were four times as likely to experience the most serious and potentially lethal violence, such as threats, assault with a gun or a knife, choking, and sexual assault. Women who experienced violence were three times as likely to report suffering a physical injury and twice as likely to report chronic ongoing assaults, defined as more than 10 separate incidents. With respect to personal safety, women victims were five times as likely to report that they feared for their lives.

Although the prevalence of domestic violence will be debated for another generation, it is clear that the impact of divorce cannot be meaningfully researched without considering violence and abuse. Numerous divorce studies that ask women why they ended their relationship find rates of domestic violence well above the rates in the general population. In most of these studies, there is no obvious motive for the participants to exaggerate the level of violence. Some divorce researchers never ask about violence and the issues are ignored; they conclude that divorce per se results in long-term adjustment problems. Other researchers, however, uncover alarming rates of abuse. By asking specific questions about the nature and severity of the violence, these researchers make obvious links to the effect of the violence on children.

The discussion of divorce in the context of domestic violence helps unravel the differential research findings on children's adjustment. For example, a recent book, *The Unexpected Legacy of Divorce* (Wallerstein, Lewis, & Blakeslee, 2000) raises the possibility that there is long-term damage to all children who experience divorce. Any separating parent reading the *Time* magazine feature on the book may worry they have forever compromised their children's adjustment. Other authors argue that the negative impact of divorce on children is exaggerated and confounded by children's predivorce problems and parental conflict (e.g., Kelly, 2000). For example, a recent study of more than 2,500 children of divorce suggest that the vast majority (75–80%) adapt to changing circumstances and are well-adjusted (Hetherington & Kelly, 2002).

In our view, one of the central problems omitted in these studies is a full discussion of domestic violence. When domestic violence is not properly addressed in the popular media, abused women may come to believe that staying with their batterer is better for their children because of the harm of separation. The conclusions are different when domestic violence and divorce are studied together. In these circumstances, some researchers have found that divorce can improve the adjustment of children and adults, and can even save lives (e.g., Jaffe & Geffner, 1998).

Is Domestic Violence Exaggerated?

Some people still feel the need to debate the accuracy of domestic violence statistics. Fathers' rights groups believe that the statistics are exaggerated and paint all men as potential batterers. Frontline shelter staff and women's advocates believe that the statistics are an inadequate measure of the scope and nature of the problem. There is less disagreement about the more severe forms of violence reported to the police or validated by court findings. At the extreme, the statistics are indisputable when violence results in death. In the United States, Canada, Australia, New Zealand, and around the world, women are far more likely than men to be killed by their intimate partner. For example, of the 1,830 domestic homicides in the United States in 1998, 75% of them had a female victim. In fact, 33% of all female murder victims were killed by intimate partners, compared with 4% of male victims (Rennison & Welchans, 2000).

In Canada, the number of domestic homicides has been decreasing for the past 10 years. In 1999, 71 men and women were killed at the hands of their intimate marriage or common-law partner. Proportionately, women were three times more likely to be killed by their husbands than men were to be killed by their wives. When the definition of intimate partner is expanded to include current or former boyfriends, then a total of 77 Canadian women were killed in their intimate relationships in 1999 (Statistics Canada, 2000a).

The spousal homicide rate in the United States over the past 25 years has reflected a definite trend when analyzed by gender. In the mid-1970s, the number of women who killed their male partners was not notably different than the number of men who killed their female partners. Since that time, there has been a steady and consistent decrease in number of men killed by their female partners, falling from 1,357 in 1976 to 424 in 1999 (Bureau of Justice Statistics, 2001). This obvious statistical trend begs the question "why?" A plausible hypothesis could relate to the increased availability of services for battered women. Over the past 25 years, women's advocates have struggled to have the concerns of battered women heard and responded to, by way of service provision, changes in police policies, and new legislation. These efforts have reduced that number of male intimate homicide victims by creating more options for battered women, who no longer see killing their batterers as their only choice. This conclusion is supported by the overwhelming evidence from domestic violence fatality reviews that female perpetrators of intimate homicides are often long-term victims of abuse inflicted on them by the men they kill (Websdale, Town, & Johnson, 1999).

When domestic violence ends in murder, there is no doubt about the dangers of separation. Fatality reviews and inquests around the world point dramatically to the increased risk when abused women and children attempt to leave their batterer (Office of the Chief Coroner, 1998; Miami-Dade County Domestic Violence Fatality Review Team, 2000). In 1996, the rate of spousal homicide for separated women was 79 per one million, compared with 3 per one million for married women (Johnson & Bunge, 2001). This statistic clearly suggests that separation can be a particularly dangerous time for women, which is consistent with the definition of domestic violence as abuse of power and control. In the 2000 Canadian Centre for Justice Statistics study, respondents were asked about domestic violence in previous unions: 28.5% of women and 21.9% of men reported violence by a previous partner (Canadian Centre for Justice Statistics, 2000). These higher rates for women may have resulted from the increased vulnerability associated with separation. Separation sends a clear message to the batterer that he is no longer in control of the relationship and his partner. His sense of loss of control is compounded by his concern about possibly losing a relationship with the children. Given that custody disputes often occur during this particularly dangerous window of time, the safety of the children and mother must be given priority and not be compromised by second-guessing the mother's motives for expressing fears for her own life and the lives of her children.

Why Do They Stay?

Many people still feel that it is reasonable to ask a battered woman why she stays in the relationship. Yet the literature available suggests that the more appropriate question is: How do battered women ever manage to leave? The authors have had numerous clients who, after leaving their batterers, have concluded it would have been better to stay with their ex-spouse than to fight the family court system and uninformed professionals, and endure many years of custody litigation.

Women who leave are often revictimized. Some authors have concluded that women are held to a higher standard of parenting and are much more likely to be held accountable for abuse, even when they are the victim. In many jurisdictions, the child protection system has been accused of blaming mothers for failing to protect children rather than holding the batterer accountable for the perpetration of his violence (Echlin & Osthoff, 2000).

Women stay in abusive relationships for many rational reasons. Some authors suggest that women engage in an ongoing and complex cost-benefit analysis that weighs safety, the needs of the children, the hope for change in the batterer, and alternative means of survival (Dutton, 1992, 1996). Individual factors such as love, fear, economic dependency, isolation, and religious convictions intermingle to create an invisible prison around the matrimonial home. Children are often a factor in women both leaving and staying. Some research suggests that a woman may decide to stay in an abusive relationship believing that the children are better off with a father who is periodically abusive to her than with no father at all. It is often overlooked by outsiders that battering men are not abusive 24 hours a day, 7 days a week. During nonviolent periods, women tend to weigh the child-focused, positive behavior of their abusive partners more significantly than the abuse they experienced the previous evening, and believe that their children benefit from the paternal relationship.

In their attempts to survive, many abused women are unwilling to acknowledge that their partner's violence against them is harmful to their children. This precarious balancing act tends to vanish with the first incident of aggression or sexual abuse directed toward the children. At that point, it is for the children's sake that many women begin to strategize about how to leave the relationship safely. Caution needs to be exercised regarding the research in this area as it is difficult to capture the complexity of the decision to leave and how this decision evolves over time.

Other Victims of Intimate Violence

Although the discussion thus far has largely focused on women as victims of abuse, men can also be victims of domestic violence at the hands of their female partners. In circumstances where a woman's violence is not motivated by self-defense, the detrimental effects on male victims need to be recognized (Cook, 1997); men may hesitate to acknowledge their victimization out of embarrassment or shame. Domestic violence can also occur in same-sex relationships—another underreported form of victimization (Cruz & Firestone, 1998; Leeder, 1988). Men or women in same-sex relationships have the double burden of disclosing their sexual orientation when they are seeking services for their victimization.

Although we recognize the existence of domestic violence in various kinds of intimate relationships, our focus is on the more common form of male violence against intimate female partners. Notwithstanding this focus, the authors do not condone the use of violence in any relationship. Our analysis about the impact of domestic violence and subsequent custody and parenting arrangements applies whenever an intimate partner is victimized.

The Politics of Domestic Violence

No discussion of domestic violence is complete without acknowledging that this is a very controversial and highly politicized topic.

Many laypeople as well as professionals believe that domestic violence is exaggerated as a means of bolstering custody claims in family law proceedings, excusing criminal conduct in criminal proceedings, or gaining financial or property settlements in civil proceedings. This view is especially prevalent in civil law, where every claim must be scrutinized and proven by the preponderance of evidence, and, therefore, any claims of abuse are viewed with suspicion and cynicism. Cynicism is particularly rampant among mental health and legal professionals who deal regularly with disturbing violent behavior. In comparison with these behaviors, the more common acts of domestic violence such as pushing, slapping, and threatening may appear insignificant. In many ways, the frequent debate between domestic violence advocates and legal/mental health professionals is based on the differing realities of this problem. One group is seeing the iceberg from under water, whereas the other group is examining the tip of the iceberg with a microscope.

The genesis of this controversy begins with the very theories used to explain domestic violence. Less controversial theories include social learning theory and family systems, or interaction, theory (Healy, Smith, & O'Sullivan, 1998). These theories posit that violence develops through early learning experiences that are reinforced by family, peer, and media exposure. Interaction theory suggests that violence must be analyzed from the perspective of family relationships, without there being a clear victim and perpetrator. More controversial is the explanation of domestic violence based on feminist theory and gender analysis. Feminist theory identifies the roots of violence in a patriarchal society wherein women's inequality and society's tolerance of male violence is commonplace—especially in the context of intimate relationships. Within these relationships, men have historically been given the right to punish or discipline their partners as harshly as they deem appropriate (Dobash & Dobash, 1992). Many feminists do not approve of the term "family violence" because it removes a gender analysis from the discussion. A phrase such as "violence against women and children" is considered, by feminists, a more accurate descriptor of the reality of violence experienced within the home (Kane, 2000).

There is agreement between feminists and nonfeminists that women are more likely to be victims of violence within their intimate relationships; both groups recognize that men may also be victims of violence. The debate concerns the nature of the victimization. Domestic violence advocates argue that women's victimization leads to more fear, more severe injuries, and higher risk of homicide, and is also more costly to society in ways that can be readily measured such as hospital, employment, and policing costs (Johnson & Burge, 2001). This discussion has created a tremendous backlash and accusations from fathers' rights groups that courts are now discriminating against fathers (Braver & O'Connell, 1998). Within the court system, judges face the formidable challenge of taking concerns about domestic violence seriously while simultaneously avoiding the perception that they are taking sides. Within this polarized and impassioned context, every allegation of violence is viewed as a malicious one and every shove is indicative of a pattern of battering.

The debate around domestic violence and child custody is summarized in Table 1.1. It is impossible to be involved in this field as a professional or lay observer without encountering the different perspectives outlined in the table. Rather than avoid entering into the discussion, efforts should be made to learn about the competing points as well as the information available in this field. As is clear from Table 1.1, there is an enormous chasm between the fundamental beliefs of fathers' rights advocates and domestic violence advocates.

Table 1.1 Fathers' Rights Groups and Domestic Violence Advocates

Issue	*Fathers' Rights Groups*	*Domestic Violence Advocates*
Postseparation parenting arrangements	Shared parenting is best	Shared parenting endangers abused women
Prevalence of domestic violence	Domestic violence is exaggerated	Domestic violence is underreported
Nature of violence	Women are as violent as men	Male violence is more severe, more injurious, and causes greater risk to life
Allegations of domestic violence	Allegations are false, used to bolster custody claims	Mothers are punished for raising allegations and counteraccused of being alienators
Family court bias	Bias against men	Bias against women and domestic violence

Polarization around these issues is rapidly increasing. Although the women's movement toiled for decades to raise public awareness about issues such as domestic violence, the fathers' rights movement has succeeded in bringing its agenda to the forefront with relative lightning speed. Politicians, legislators, and policymakers are bombarded with diametrically opposed viewpoints as to how the family court system should be reformed. The cry of bias in the courts has been heard across North America. In one corner, fathers' rights groups argue that fathers are being stripped of involvement in their children's lives post-separation. In the other corner, domestic violence advocates warn that court orders of joint custody and liberal visitation are compromising the safety of women and children. The net effect is that many in this field, whether judges, assessors, arbitrators, or guardians ad litem, are being immobilized by the prospect of accusations of bias. Any suggested parenting plan that does not divide children's care time equally may be defined as prejudicial and/or unfair toward mothers or fathers. Helping professionals, in large numbers, have been ensnared by this definition of fairness. They erroneously believe that considering the relevance of domestic violence is tantamount to being partisan to mothers.

In Canada, a joint Commons-Senate committee travelled across the country in 1998 seeking input from communities on amendments to the Divorce Act. The hearings resulted in "gender wars," with fathers' rights supporters hissing and booing when some presenters raised issues of domestic violence within custody disputes (Bala, 1999). Newspaper headlines championed fathers' rights messages that allegations of child abuse and domestic violence are false, that fathers are commonly denied contact with their children post-separation, and that alienation on the part of mothers is a pervasive problem. Clearly, the determination of the "best interest" of the child in a custody dispute exists within a highly charged and politicized context.

❖ HIGH-CONFLICT CUSTODY DISPUTES

Most parents separate with little formal intervention from the legal system (Johnston, 1994). This basic reality is often overlooked by professionals whose daily working lives are absorbed by highly acrimonious divorcing couples. Such professionals may lose sight of the continuum of couples who separate. Parents engaged in perpetual litigation are not representative of all divorcing couples. The majority of separating parents resolve their differences through sound advice from friends and family that keeps them focused on the needs of their children. They may require minimal to no services from lawyers and mediators to arrive at a mutually agreeable postseparation parenting plan. In some cases, there is no conflict because one parent may leave the jurisdiction and abandon all parenting rights and obligations.

Approximately one in five divorces requires more intensive intervention, often in the form of family, or civil, litigation. For these families, the resources utilized may be extensive. Commonly, these cases appear numerous times before the court, over prolonged periods of time. The services of arbitrators, assessors, and/or guardians ad litem are requested. Lawyers may submit numerous motions and affidavits, in an effort to capture their client's version of reality on paper. These cases—with the accompanying court appearances, threats, letters of complaint, and resource depletion—are the ones most familiar to family court judges and court-appointed evaluators.

The children of these divorces are most at risk for serious adjustment problems because of the severe conflict that envelops their daily lives. Decisions about schools, medical care, extracurricular activities, and religion may become an extended battleground. The divorce literature describes these cases as "high-conflict." There is burgeoning literature to assist legal and mental health professionals to resolve high-conflict custody disputes. Increasingly, this literature recognizes that these families do not benefit from the basic services available to divorcing couples such as parent education programs, mediation, and divorce counselling.

There is general agreement that these high-conflict cases require unique strategies on the part of legal and mental health professionals before any meaningful resolution can occur. Rather than empowering parents to resolve their conflicts, stringent guidelines are imposed on parents in the best interests of their children. The focus in these cases shifts to separate parenting relationships; cooperative co-parenting, frequent transitions, and joint custody are not deemed appropriate. In fact, the children from these high-conflict families tend to experience more emotional and behavioral difficulties when transitions occur frequently. In many of these cases, the reality is that no viable resolution exists. The focus is on developing a management plan to protect the children from parental conflict, and to ration court-related services and resources (Johnston, 1994; Johnston & Roseby, 1997).

An essential principle from the high-conflict divorce area is that joint custody and shared parenting plans are not viable resolutions. One of the most renowned authors in the field, Dr. Janet Johnston, has written extensively about the specialized needs of high-conflict families. She suggests that any notion of joint custody be abandoned and replaced with very clear custody and visitation plans, limiting the parents' opportunity for renewed hostilities that would compromise children's postseparation adjustment. Flexibility in the plan is viewed as fanning the flame for ongoing conflict. In these cases, the custody and visitation plans must not only consider the developmental needs of the children but also the nature and severity of the parental conflict. Increased severity calls for decreased flexibility. Visitation plans must safeguard both the mother's and the children's physical well-being. Recommended interventions include supervised transfers, less frequent visitation, and exchanges in neutral places such as schools to avoid parental contact.

Specific postseparation parenting plans have been developed that take into account children's stages of development as well as the degree of conflict between the parents. These guidelines can be very helpful to those grappling with decisions about children's postseparation care time. For example, Garrity and Baris developed excellent guidelines for children of varying ages whose parents have minimal to severe conflict. Suggested parenting plans vary in accordance with both variables and highlight the necessity of tailoring plans in the best interests of the children (Garrity & Baris, 1994).

High-conflict custody disputes can exist without domestic violence. Some divorcing parents hate each other with such intensity that they are prepared to invest unlimited legal and emotional resources to prove what a terrible person the other parent is. These disputes are often fuelled by financial considerations, jealousy about new partners, the need to be vindicated as superior, or serious personality and/or mental disorders.

Imbedded within this population of high-conflict families are cases where domestic violence is a central factor. There is some controversy about the very language used to describe these circumstances, as domestic violence advocates believe that the term "high-conflict" minimizes the insidious and profound nature of the domestic violence.

Nonetheless, research on high-conflict families offers an important bridge linking the domestic violence field with divorce and separation. If high-conflict families demand unique postseparation remedies to reduce children's adjustment difficulties and exposure to conflict, then cases involving domestic violence must require similar solutions.

At the same time, there are special considerations involved in high-conflict custody disputes in which domestic violence is present. In some of these cases, it may be appropriate to require supervised visitation or no visitation at all. These cases are a special challenge for judges who, in their compassion for fathers, may compromise children's safety out of a genuinely held belief that children benefit from a relationship with their parent no matter how abusive they appear. Judges may also hold naive beliefs about how quickly batterers can change their behavior and interactional style. In the absence of overwhelming evidence of abuse or expert testimony about abusive relationships, the courts may be swayed by the passionate pleas and promises by fathers to change their behaviors. Batterers, by their very nature, excel at misrepresenting themselves in this environment.

It is unfortunate that the fathers' rights movement has emerged just as society is beginning to acknowledge that there is no quick fix to the complex issue of divorce and domestic violence. Fathers' rights advocates have successfully put simplistic solutions at the forefront of public pressure and political debate, much to the disservice of victimized mothers and their children. The fathers' rights movement has been packaged and presented as the consolidated male perspective of the family court system. Although these right-wing groups are often representative of only a smattering of devotees, some suggest that the agenda of the fathers' rights movement is the only one with a real influence on the media, political debate, and law reform (Kaye & Tolmie, 1998).

❖ CUSTODY DISPUTES AND DOMESTIC VIOLENCE

Family courts have traditionally turned a blind eye to domestic violence or have minimized its significance. Custody disputes involving domestic violence have been forced into a one-size-fits-all paradigm, an erroneous and potentially life-threatening approach. What is required is a differentiated approach based on careful screening of cases for the presence of domestic violence and thoughtful consideration of the clinical and legal implications. These cases need specialized resources and well-trained professionals to ensure that victims of domestic violence and their children are not revictimized by a justice system designed to protect them. Ironically, at a time when there is growing public awareness of domestic violence, the family law system has been one of the least responsive institutions to this social problem.

Women who raise concerns about a violent partner in family court proceedings are unlikely to be believed because lawyers and judges tend to overemphasize the possibility that false allegations are being used to further custody claims. Certainly there is the possibility that false allegations are being lodged; however, much more common are false denials by actual perpetrators of violence. The overwhelming reality is that victims of domestic violence are far more likely to cover up, minimize, and deny their abusive experiences than to lodge false allegations. Yet genuine batterers routinely denounce their accuser and commonly retaliate with accusations that their partners are actually the aggressors, are unfit, or are systematically brainwashing the children.

The combination of batterers' predictable counter-allegations and the courts' vigilance with respect to false allegations creates a perilous situation for victims of domestic violence. As a result, domestic violence advocates regard the family court system as a real and potential source of incredible revictimization. Their view is that too many women leave life-threatening situations with their children only to find that there is no refuge. Many professionals remain skeptical about the reality of battered women's experiences. Domestic violence victims, especially at a point of crisis, are hardly equipped to deal with the emotional and cognitive challenges involved in traversing the legal labyrinth. Many times they cannot supply the evidence to support their claim. Even when they do, judges and lawyers may not find it relevant to determining issues related to custody and visitation (Jaffe & Geffner, 1998). Clearly, high-conflict custody disputes, in particular when there is domestic violence, require the very best resources that the justice system has to offer. The delivery of these resources demands thoughtful, sensitive, and well-coordinated services to ensure that children's safety and healing are at the forefront.

Victimized women must not only contend with a complex and, at times, hostile court system but must also manage their fear that the batterer will carry out his threats. Many battered women report that their ex-partners threatened to obtain custody of the children after separation as a means of ensuring their silence and compliance within the relationship. Some batterers incessantly remind their spouse that their charm, believability, or tenacity will successfully convince the court of their superiority in family court proceedings. Although some batterers genuinely want a relationship with their children and desire an improved postseparation relationship, many batterers pursue visitation as a way of gaining access to their ex-partner. They may seek custody and engage in prolonged litigation, during which their legal counsel and the court process mirrors the dynamics of the abusive relationship. For many women, the burden of battling their former partner, traversing a court system that is highly suspicious of allegations of violence, and coping with a visitation schedule that delivers their children into the arms of their abuser can be crushing.

In the majority of cases, when women and children escape an abusive situation, the road to recovery is filled with challenges to their physical and emotional well-being. Many authors have linked surviving abuse with posttraumatic stress disorder (PTSD), which, at the extreme, contributes to the development of a complex array of debilitating symptoms (Herman, 1992) that can alter an individual's personality and worldview. On the less severe end of the continuum, survivors of intimate abuse may suffer from anxiety, depression, low self-esteem, inability to trust future partners, and sexual dysfunction. In light of these challenges, the expectations that the legal system imposes on survivors of domestic violence to be a "friendly parent," to mediate "differences," or "move on with life and put the past behind you" can appear insurmountable. The problems previously outlined may also be compounded by such life stressors as poverty, racism, classism, disabilities, language barriers, undocumented status, and lack of access to needed services.

The literature on high-conflict resolution strategies and remedies can be applicable to cases involving domestic violence. Proposed solutions in high-conflict cases are consistent with many of the recommendations offered by domestic violence advocates to address the needs of abused women and children. As a prime example, many organizations have recommended that a finding of domestic violence should create a presumption that the perpetrators of the violence not have sole or joint custody of children. This premise has been endorsed by national organizations such as the National Council of Juvenile and Family Court Judges, the American Psychological Association, and the American Bar Association. The U.S. Congress, over a decade ago, passed a resolution that declared,

> It is the sense of Congress that, for the purposes of determining child custody, credible evidence of physical abuse of a spouse should create a statutory presumption that it is detrimental to the child to be placed in the custody of the abusive spouse . . . . There is an alarming bias against battered spouses in contemporary child custody trends such as joint custody. . . . Joint custody guarantees the batterer continued access and control over the battered spouse's life through their children. . . . Joint custody, forced upon hostile parents, can create a dangerous psychological environment for a child. (Morella, 1990, p. S18252-04)

In Canada, there has been considerable debate about divorce laws and how to create more consistency between federal divorce legislation and various provincial laws dealing with separation. Domestic violence is recognized by a number of significant judgements, but it has not been enshrined in legislation as a factor for courts weighing custody decisions. During the hearings of the Joint Commons Senate Committee, fathers' rights groups sought to replace the term "custody" with "shared parenting." In response, a number of legal scholars and domestic violence organizations argued that adopting such a plan would deny the reality of many domestic violence victims fighting for their children's safety (Bala, 2000). The obvious resolution is to recognize different remedies for different family disputes, validating both ends of this continuum. However, the debate is further polarized by those who argue that domestic violence is an exaggerated problem and advocate criminal consequences for "false" allegations of abuse. There is tremendous pressure on federal and provincial justice ministers to find a meaningful solution that addresses these complex issues. Unsophisticated and ill-informed solutions will inevitably jeopardize the psychological and physical health of children.

Custody Dispute Myths and Misnomers

It is a widely held belief that mothers have an overwhelming advantage in custody disputes and that fathers have a slim chance of maintaining meaningful contact with their children post-separation. Many mental health professionals and lawyers who have been involved in custody disputes where domestic violence is a factor challenge this perception. Their experiences are that battered women regularly face significant obstacles as they find their way through family court proceedings. Recent research suggests that in cases where domestic violence is an issue, batterers are actually more likely to obtain visitation rights than nonviolent fathers. In a study by O'Sullivan (2000), over 2,000 cases in which visitation petitions were filed in New York City and Westchester County were randomly chosen and analyzed with respect to visitation orders and protection orders. In both jurisdictions, fathers who had protection orders against them had a much higher probability of being granted visitation compared with those fathers who never had a protection order against them. The highest probability for visitation occurred in the cases where the fathers asked for a protection order against the mother (O'Sullivan, 2000). Zorza's review of the literature and patterns of court judgments also suggests that batterers have surprisingly high success rates in convincing judges of the merits of their case for custody (Zorza, 1995).

In our extensive experience with disputed custody cases, abusive husbands appear to take a degree of pleasure from the "gamesplaying" of court proceedings. They often seek outcomes in which they have no genuine interest. As an example, they may demand custody or extensive visitation rights with no history of parenting or having time available for the children. Some fathers who pursue lengthy litigation may be less interested in contact with their children than in engaging their ex-partner in legal warfare. It has been suggested that batterers are overrepresented in highly litigious custody cases and that the motive is to prolong their control over, intimidation of, and involvement with their ex-partners; the children are no more than a means to an end (Zorza, 1995).

Sinclair (2000) conducted focus groups with 52 women who were engaged in custody proceedings and were victims of domestic violence. Of this group of 52 women, 88% reported that their children had been present during their abuse and 79% reported that the children were directly abused by their ex-partner. The findings indicate that the average length of time to resolve the dispute was 3.5 years, with some cases lasting in excess of 6.5 years before resolution was reached. In 74% of the cases, mothers were awarded sole custody and their ex-partners were awarded unsupervised access. In 20% of the cases, the abusive partner was awarded joint custody. In 6% of the cases, supervised access was awarded to the perpetrator of domestic violence. Domestic violence and prolonged custody litigation is harmful to abused women. The children who grow up within these homes are also adversely affected. The next section will highlight this developing area of the literature.

❖ IMPACT OF DOMESTIC VIOLENCE ON CHILDREN

Emery was among the first researchers to identify conflict as the active harmful ingredient for children coping with divorce. According to his research, and that of other social science researchers, children show the greatest level of adjustment difficulties when their parents' separation is marked by conflict before, during, and after the relationship ends. The concept that divorce per se did not result in emotional and behavior problems but, rather, that the problems came from exposure to severe conflict was a novel idea (Emery, 1982).

Obviously, embedded in the word "conflict" is a range of behaviors that includes domestic violence. Subsequent researchers have focused on the effect of exposure to domestic violence on children. Historically, children were viewed as unscathed if they themselves were not directly abused. However, growing research in this area has demonstrated the very opposite to be true. Researchers such as Edleson, Jaffe, and others have identified a host of behavioral, emotional, and psychological difficulties associated with exposure to domestic violence. In general, this research suggests that exposure to parental violence is a form of psychological abuse and can be harmful to children both in the short term and over their life span. As with any other trauma or life stressor, how children are affected individually is dependent on a range of variables including their age, gender, the presence of other risk factors, and protective factors such as an extensive support system and access to resources that may reduce the harm they suffer (Rossman, Hughes, & Rosenberg, 2000).

Over the past decade, considerable research has been conducted that highlights the extensive impact of exposure to violence on children. This field is still in its infancy with many outstanding questions regarding the mediators of short-term and long-term adjustment. Readers who desire a more in-depth analysis of the debates and research findings to date are encouraged to explore several outstanding contributions in the literature (e.g., Rossman et al., 2000; Graham-Bermann & Edleson, 2001; Holden, Geffner, & Jouriles, 2001; Geffner, Jaffe, & Sudermann, 2000).

This section distills some of the major findings and current controversies in the field related to children's symptoms, influence of age and gender, as well as what is known about possible risk and protective factors. The important caution in reviewing this literature as a whole is that there is great variability in how a particular child may cope with exposure to violence. Data gathered from groups of children who have been exposed to parental violence identifies important themes for clinical practice and future research. However, this data may not predict how an individual child may deal with his or her unique circumstances. For example, a child may excel academically because school has been a safe and enriching haven from the violence in the family. However, other children may pose serious behavioral management problems within the classroom, thereby compounding their violence-related difficulties with academic and social deterioration.

Some children may be exposed to extreme violence and still mature into professionally successful adults, such as former U.S. President Bill Clinton and author Gavin De Becker (*The Gift of Fear;* De Becker, 1997). Other children may be exposed to less severe and less frequent forms of spousal violence, but be profoundly affected because of the presence of other risk factors, such as isolation, learning disabilities, or self-blaming. In short, each child is affected in a unique manner when forced to cope with domestic violence in his or her family. Two children in the same family may respond very differently to the same level of violence, depending on a host of complicated interacting variables that we are only beginning to appreciate. There is a need for more sophisticated research in this area that examines children's adjustment as a function of risk and resiliency factors, together with a conceptual framework to guide future analyses (Jaffe, Poisson, & Cunningham, 2001).

With that caution expressed, the following synopsis outlines what the research to date has identified as possible adjustment problems faced by children exposed to domestic violence. These children may exhibit a wide variety of symptoms, including the following.

Aggressive and Noncompliant Behavior. Children may become aggressive with siblings, peers, and teachers. They can be noncompliant, irritable, and easily angered. Some children who destroy property and have a tendency to get into fights may develop more antisocial behavior in their adolescence and end up in Juvenile Court as offenders.

Emotional and Internalizing Problems. Emotional (internalizing) problems such as anxiety, depression, low self-esteem, withdrawal, and lethargy are also noted in children who are exposed to family violence. Other children experience somatic complaints (bodily aches, pains, and illness with no known medical cause). These symptoms may result because the children have a lot of internal tension, with no effective way of addressing the problem, expressing their feelings, or seeking help. Many observers have felt that internalizing problems, along with a need to be perfectly behaved, and an exaggerated sense of needing to help their mother are particularly common in girls who witness family violence (Jaffe, Wolfe, & Wilson, 1990; Kerig, Fedorowicz, Brown, Patenaude, & Warren, 1998).

Effects on Social and Academic Development. Some studies have shown that children who witness domestic violence may be hampered in their social and school development (Moore, Pepler, Mae, & Michele, 1989; Randolf & Talamo, 1997). Children who have been exposed to violence may be preoccupied with this issue and have difficulty concentrating on schoolwork. Their social development may be hampered because they are too sad, anxious, or preoccupied to participate in social activities. Some children may use aggressive strategies in interpersonal problem solving that may make them unpopular and rejected. Some community workers have noted that some young women from culturally diverse immigrant groups who live in violent homes may hurry through their education, striving for an early but culturally approved means of escape from the family setting, such as an early marriage, or taking a job before they have achieved all they could have in terms of educational level (Kazarian & Kazarian, 1998).

Posttraumatic Stress Disorder. Recent studies have shown that many children who witness domestic violence suffer from PTSD. These children have been exposed to violence involving serious injury or death threats. The children's response involved acute fear, helplessness, or horror; or in the case of younger children, agitated or disorganized behavior. In addition, the domestic violence is re-experienced (e.g., through nightmares). There may be a persistent avoidance of anything that reminds the child of the violence. Symptoms of increased arousal, such as difficulty falling asleep, irritability, outbursts of anger, difficulty concentrating, hypervigilance, and an exaggerated startle response may be present (see PTSD criteria in *DSM-IV-TR,* American Psychiatric Association, 2000). Lehmann found that 56% of a sample of children in women's shelters met the full criteria for PTSD and the majority of the remaining children in the sample showed some symptoms associated with this disorder (Lehmann, 1997). Similarly, Graham-Berman and Levendosky found that 13% of their sample of 64 children exposed to domestic violence qualified for a complete posttraumatic stress disorder (PTSD) diagnosis. However, 52% suffered from intrusive and unwanted remembering of the traumatic event(s), 19% displayed traumatic avoidance, and 42% experienced traumatic arousal symptoms. Children with PTSD symptoms had significantly more internalizing behavioral problems and more externalizing problems than did children without trauma symptoms (Graham-Bermann & Levendosky, 1998). Many children who are exposed to woman abuse in their homes may never have known a calm, peaceful environment, even from their earliest childhood or infancy, and, thus, their development and reactions are more chronically affected than those children who experience a single traumatic event in a peaceful and supportive environment.

Subtle Symptoms. Frequently, there are also more subtle symptoms related to children exposed to violence, such as inappropriate attitudes about the use of violence in resolving conflicts; inappropriate attitudes about violence against women; condoning violence in intimate and dating relationships; hypersensitivity about problems at home; and a sense that they are to blame for the violence.

Children and adolescents may exhibit different symptoms according to their age and stage of development when they were exposed to the violence.

Prenatal. It is common for abuse to begin or continue during the time a woman is pregnant. A 1993 survey by Statistics Canada found that 21% of women abused by a marital partner were assaulted during pregnancy, and of these women, 40% indicated the abuse began during pregnancy (Rodgers, 1994). Researchers have found that a significant number of women in routine prenatal care disclosed abuse once they were asked appropriate screening questions (McFarlane, Parker, Soeken, & Bullock, 1992). The full extent of effects of abuse on prenatal development and the intrauterine environment remain to be studied. However, women who are abused and beaten during pregnancy clearly suffer an elevated risk of injury to the fetus and complications during pregnancy and delivery.

Birth to 2 Years of Age. Even very young infants respond to witnessing parental conflict by stress that is measurable through heart rate, galvanic skin response, and overt crying and distress (Cummings, Iannotti, & Zahn-Waxler, 1985). The effects of witnessing domestic violence, in addition to the negative effects on the mother's ability to focus on and care sensitively for her infant, can result in severe attachment problems and failure to thrive by the infant. Babies are also especially at physical risk during domestic violence, as they may be hit while in their mother's arms or near their mother, or they may be thrown or hit by the abuser.

The work of Perry on the effects of violent environments on very young children suggests that permanent negative changes in the child's brain and neural development occur when a child is exposed to abuse and other forms of violence at these ages (Perry, 1995). Perry states that exposure to traumatic violence will alter the developing central nervous system, predisposing the individual to more impulsive, reactive, and violent behavior. Some of the behavioral results at later ages may include hypervigilance to perceived threats and overresponsivity (aggression) when aggressive acts by others are anticipated. Although further research is required in this area, the research does point to the serious nature of exposure by infants and young children to domestic violence.

Preschoolers. Preschoolers, like infants, are severely distressed by witnessing abuse and conflict between their parents. Even relatively mild conflict causes toddlers to cease playing and exploring, look distressed, seek proximity to their mother, and become very upset. Another effect is that some toddlers will imitate the behavior by lashing out at playmates and siblings (Cummings & Davies, 1994). Preschoolers who witness severe violence are often very clingy, have anxious attachments with their mothers, are difficult to manage, and are negative in their mood. Assessing trauma in preschool-aged children is considered controversial because their symptoms may be quite different from adults who are diagnosed with PTSD. For example, these children are likely to show signs of hyperarousal, rather than symptoms of avoidance (Levendosky, Huth Bocks, Semel, & Shapiro, 2002).

School Children Aged 6 to 11. Children in the earlier school years often show their distress at witnessing domestic violence in aggressive and/or withdrawn behavior at school and difficulty in concentrating at school (Jaffe et al., 1990). These are the children who are often labeled with attention deficit disorder, without first being asked questions about what they are witnessing at home. Difficulties with peer relationships are often apparent, as well as low self-esteem and lack of energy for participation in school (Moore et al., 1989). Boys may begin to be especially defiant with female teachers, mimicking the disrespect for women they see at home. Overall, children in this age group who are exposed to domestic violence tend to show both emotional and behavioral problems (Sternberg et al., 1993), although individual children will vary in their symptom severity because of factors such as frequency, severity, and duration of violence witnessed; personality and family characteristics; and strengths and coping abilities.

Adolescents. Adolescents who witness domestic violence may become truant at school because of anxiety and wanting to stay home as a protector for the victimized parent. Some adolescents cope through alcohol and drug abuse or escape the family situation by running away from home. Involvement in juvenile delinquency occurs at an elevated rate. A lack of ability to focus on future plans is often present, together with an avoidance style of coping. Depression and suicide is another possibility at this age. Involvement with an antisocial peer group is common. The most common and specific indicator of exposure to domestic violence may be abusive dating relationships in adolescents who begin to practice what they have witnessed at home (Reitzel & Wolfe, 2001).

Adult Effects. Some research suggests long-term negative effects of exposure to domestic violence. For example, a number of studies have found that exposure to family violence in childhood predicts less positive adult social adjustment (Henning, Leitenberg, Coffey, Turner, & Bennett, 1996) and depression in adulthood (Straus, 1992). In travel and public speaking about these issues, we have met countless adults who are still haunted by childhood memories of domestic violence. These individuals often disclose lifelong symptoms such as distrust of any intimate relationship and ongoing flashbacks and nightmares.

The most common adult effect may be the cycle of violence, which refers to the fact that childhood exposure to violence is one of the significant factors associated with domestic violence in adult years (Reitzel & Wolfe, 2001).

A more detailed overview of these consequences of exposure to domestic violence in children and adolescents, as well as the implications for parents and social service and health care providers, is available through the senior author's organization (Sudermann & Jaffe, 1999).

Risk and Protective Factors

Increasingly, researchers are interested in accounting for individual differences when children are exposed to similarly traumatic events. Risk and protective factors are essential elements in understanding the variability in children's behavior. Although this book focuses on domestic violence and child-custody disputes, the research in risk and protective factors spans a wide range of traumas children may experience. For example, in the child sexual abuse literature, considerable research has been conducted on the dimensions of abuse as well as the disclosure process and the response from supportive family members and community professionals. Without oversimplifying the findings, the research suggests that the impact of the abuse is moderated by factors inherent in the child (e.g., intelligence and temperament), the family environment (the presence of supportive adults, or the presence of other forms of maltreatment), and community response (the safety of the child and victimized parent is the priority for community services). In the same way, domestic violence occurs in the context of unique child characteristics, family dynamics, and community resources.

Within the domestic violence field, the risk and protective factors mentioned in Table 1.2 appear to have some significance.

Table 1.2 Risk and Protective Factors

Risk Factors	*Protective Factors*
• Presence of parental mental health challenges • Presence of parental substance abuse • Poverty and lack of access to resources (housing, economic support, legal assistance, counselling, employment, child care) • Family vulnerability (recent immigration, language and cultural barriers, visible minority status, parental disabilities)	• Supportive relationship with nonabusive parent • Supportive relationship with an adult outside the immediate family • Alternative role models • Success in academic, social, or recreational pursuits • Access to resources to support child and family (responses from the CAS and police that promote safety and healing)

To summarize, an understanding of the effect of domestic violence on an individual child will develop from an analysis of these risk and protective factors as well as the nature and severity of the violence. The consequences will unfold according to the children's gender and stage of development and the unique challenges of that stage. The toddler who had mastered toilet training may regress to an earlier stage when dealing with the anxiety from the traumatic event. The teen who is developing his first intimate relationship may exhibit his problems through an abusive relationship with his girlfriend. The research in this area allows us to see trends and generate hypotheses about individual cases but only comprehensive assessments can really shed light on how each child may have responded to the violence in his or her home.

❖ WHY IS DOMESTIC VIOLENCE RELEVANT TO CHILD CUSTODY?

Our motivation to write this book grew out of our frustration that well-educated professionals working daily with families in crisis do not seem to understand the relevance of exposure to domestic violence on child adjustment. Repeatedly, these professionals express the view that children are not harmed by exposure to domestic violence, and that perpetration of spousal violence has no bearing on parenting. Even when they acknowledge the possible harm to children, these professionals minimize the potential ongoing and serious challenges to children's well-being after parental separation. In the following sections, we will highlight the major reasons why domestic violence is relevant for the determination of child-custody disputes and the best interests of children. Many mental health and legal professionals naively believe that once separation has occurred, the violence is over and children's problems are historical. From our perspective, based on our experience in the justice system and knowledge of the scientific literature, this view jeopardizes the safety of women and children. Not only is domestic violence relevant but also it should be a fundamental consideration in determining the best interest of the child postseparation.

Abuse Does Not End With Separation

Separation is not a vaccination against domestic violence. To the contrary, physical abuse, stalking, and harassment continue at significant rates post-separation. National research in Canada has suggested that for approximately one quarter of abuse victims, the violence became more severe compared with preseparation violence (Statistics Canada, 2001). Furthermore, this same study found that 39% of victims of domestic violence reported that the first incident of domestic violence occurred after separation (Statistics Canada, 2001). Other researchers have similarly found that the rate of postseparation violence is high (Liss & Stahly, 1993).

Visitation can be used by batterers as an opportunity to further abuse their former spouse. In a Canadian study (Leighton, 1989), one quarter of the women reported that their lives were threatened during visitation. Often, access to children after separation will require specialized supervision facilities to protect both the children and victimized parent from ongoing abuse (Sheeran & Hampton, 1999).

In our clinical experience, children may be frightened by their parents being at the same place (e.g., school play, pick up or drop off from a visit) even if there is no violence or threat of violence. For the adults, the violence may be over, but for the children, the past traumatic event has engendered such fear that any association with the past (e.g., the presence of both parents at the same place) can create significant anxiety and distress. Although one parent may be accused of transmitting his or her anxiety to the children, the most common reason for distress tends to be children's strong memories and feelings about past hostilities.

Child Abuse and Domestic Violence

Although many professionals are unable or unwilling to appreciate the relevance of domestic violence in determining a child's best interest, there is no debate about abuse directly inflicted on children. Increasingly, mental health practitioners and researchers are recognizing that many maltreated children and abused women come from the same homes. Recent reviews of studies across different settings and with different samples indicate that the co-occurrence of child abuse and spousal abuse is high. In an examination of nearly three dozen studies, reviewers found similar empirical findings: Between 30% and 60% of children whose mothers had experienced abuse were themselves likely to be abused (Edleson, 1999). According to recent literature reviews, there are nearly one million children who were identified by child protection services as victims of substantiated or indicated abuse or neglect and well over one million American women who were physically assaulted within the past 12 months (Weithorn, 2001). Frequently, these women and children are in the same homes.

Fear for their children's safety is an ongoing concern for battered women. In a national study conducted by the Canadian Centre for Justice Statistics, women were six times more likely than men to report being afraid for their children (Johnson & Burge, 2001) when they were victims of domestic violence.

Batterers as Poor Role Models

The family is the fundamental unit of children's socialization. Children learn powerful lessons from their parents including how to resolve conflict and how to cope with having their needs frustrated. Laboratory studies suggest that children may fail to learn how to moderate their emotions when they are exposed to their parents' anger and emotional outbursts (Cummings et al., 1985). When children witness one parent inflicting abuse on the other, or using threats of violence to maintain control within a relationship, seeds are planted that may result in the cycle repeating itself. If a father believes that he is king of his castle and the children's mother is his servant, lessons on sex-role expectations are being passed on to the children.

Research suggests that most batterers have themselves been exposed to their mothers' victimization in childhood (Straus et al., 1980). Even in adolescence, dating violence is predicted by abusive role models during childhood, which are reinforced by peer groups and societal attitudes (Reitzel & Wolfe, 2001). For younger siblings, the impact of inappropriate role models may be compounded within a family. Not only do these children have to cope with exposure to domestic violence but also they may be victimized by older siblings who have absorbed the lessons of violence. In fact, this sibling abuse may predict future violence in intimate relationships for both boys and girls (Simonelli, Mullis, Elliott, & Pierce, 2002).

Undermining of the Nonabusive Parent

Many batterers engage in alienating and blaming behavior and openly communicate this to the children. They blame the mother for ending the marriage without any acknowledgment of her right to a safe and secure home environment. The consequences of the violence in the mother—which are common trauma symptoms—are twisted by the batterer as signs that the mother is crazy, unfit, or unstable. These views are openly shared with the children. Consistent with the "Power and Control Wheel" (see page 40) developed by the Domestic Abuse Intervention Project in Duluth, Minnesota, the children become a tool to utilize in maintaining abusive power and control in the relationship even after separation. The court itself and the batterer's lawyer may inadvertently become an extension of this abuse though the legal proceedings.

Some researchers and practitioners have pointed out that the courts and court-related services often overlook the specific role of a domestic violence perpetrator as a parent (Bancroft & Silverman, 2002). The impact of a batterer goes beyond the trauma of exposure to violence and tension in a home and involves undermining the other parent's authority—retaliating to find safety, sowing divisions in the family, and using the children as a weapon (Bancroft & Silverman, 2002). These issues are rarely addressed by custody evaluators and judges.

Violence in New Relationships

Violent fathers may move on to new partners and continue to inflict abuse if there has been no meaningful intervention or accountability. One research study found that 58% of male offenders perpetrated violence against their new partners after the dissolution of a previously abusive relationship (Woffordt, Mihalic, & Menard, 1994). This high likelihood of continued violence results in ongoing exposure to abuse for children of divorce. Ironically, some judges and mental health professionals tend to view reinvolvement on the part of the male as an indicator of stability or maturation in these new relationships. In our clinical experience with child-custody cases involving domestic violence, the key witness for the father is usually a new wife or female partner who testifies to the kind and gentle manner of the batterer in this new relationship. The message to the judge is that the problem is one of interaction or the difficult mother rather than any accountability or acknowledgment for past violence.

Perpetual Litigation

The family court can be exploited by batterers as a means of continuing their abusive behavior. Through extensive litigation, which drains the emotional and financial resources of the abused woman, the batterer may draw the judge and his own counsel into his desire to maintain control of the relationship. Some authors have suggested that batterers are twice as likely as nonbatterers to apply for custody of the children and are equally likely to be successful in this pursuit (Bowermaster & Johnson, 1998; Zorza, 1995). In one study involving 52 abused women, many of them faced years of litigation in which they felt little intervention by courts to protect them from ongoing legal harassment (Sinclair, 2000).

Extreme Outcomes

At the extreme of the continuum of domestic violence cases are ones in which credible threats of abduction and homicide take place. Missing children's organizations are a monument to what desperate parents do to each other and their children. Tremendous fear and distrust is engendered just by the possibility of such action by mothers or fathers. Some of these cases involve a parent committing a willful criminal act and others appear to involve a parent seeking safety from an abusive spouse (see Chapters 3 and 4 for legal implications).

Threats of homicide are taken more seriously in this decade because of the growing literature linking domestic violence, separation, and homicide as well as the development of risk-assessment tools (Campbell, 1995; Campbell, Sharps, & Glass, 2001). Children may become involved as witnesses to homicides or as homicide victims themselves in these extreme circumstances (Websdale et al., 1999). In New Zealand, such a tragedy in which a batterer killed his three children resulted in government inquiry and legislative changes that presume that batterers will not have custody of children (Busch & Robertson, 2000).

❖ CONCLUSION

In conclusion, from a clinical and legal perspective, domestic violence is an important area of inquiry in addressing child-custody disputes. If a history of domestic violence is present, a unique analysis must follow and all the data and patterns of behavior must be weighed differently. It is as if legal and mental health professionals need a different lens through which to view the information and competing allegations in the determination of a child's best interest. Domestic violence within a custody and access case demands a paradigm shift. By way of analogy, legal and mental health professionals can be considered akin to security guards at an airport. Ninety percent of the passengers pass quickly and unfettered through the screening process without sounding the alarm, much as the vast majority of divorcing parents need minimal legal resources to resolve their postseparation parenting plan. However, when the alarm indicates the presence of metal, or an X-ray highlights an unusual shape in a piece of luggage, extra time and care is required to conduct a more thorough search. Similarly, when parents express concerns about their safety and their children's safety, the dangers must be more closely examined.

Clearly, one size does not fit all families in custody disputes. Lawyers, judges, and mental health professionals need to ensure that the right interventions are matched to the right clients. Some of the best developments of the late 1900s, such as mediation and joint custody, are not appropriate solutions to child-custody disputes involving domestic violence. Just as an airport security guard can jeopardize the welfare of all passengers by ignoring warning alarms, legal and mental health professionals who ignore warning signs of domestic violence can endanger the lives of children and parents by minimizing, denying, or excusing the reality of domestic violence.

The approach to this problem requires care and competence, lest the issue of domestic violence be dismissed or overshadowed by concerns centering on "false allegations." The advances in this field are occurring at a time when there is considerable backlash about recognizing violence in the family. There are still many professionals who are skeptical about the prevalence of domestic violence and equally likely to suspect that mothers are raising violence allegations to further their custody claims and associated financial support. Sometimes mothers are accused of using a history of domestic violence to deflect concerns about their parenting abilities.

At the extreme, some professionals believe that a significant number of mothers actively try to ruin the relationship between fathers and children through conscious and willful alienation. These views have been fueled by the concept of parent alienation syndrome (PAS), espoused by psychiatrist Richard Gardner, over the past 20 years (Gardner, 1992). Although PAS has no scientific foundation to support the reliability and validity of such a label (Faller, 1998; Kerr & Jaffe, 1998), it has nonetheless been embraced by several groups and uncritical mental and legal professionals. This issue will be addressed in more detail in Chapter 2.

This opening chapter conveys the importance of considering domestic violence within the context of disputed child-custody cases. Some authors would argue that the determination of child custody is so complex that it would be unfair to place too much weight on any one factor such as domestic violence (Stahl, 1994). The authors feel strongly that domestic violence has been widely overlooked and minimized in this field. We believe that it is imperative that we centralize our focus on those child-custody cases in which domestic violence is a legitimate factor in the best interest of the children and the safety and well-being of family members. In the next chapter, we turn our attention to issues related to assessing children and parents in these complex clinical and legal proceedings.

2

Assessing Safety and Responsibility in Child-Custody Disputes

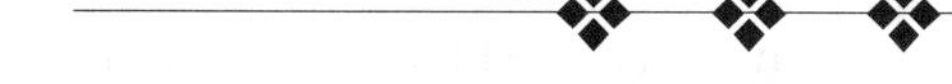

❖ ASSESSING DOMESTIC VIOLENCE ISSUES

Legal and mental health professionals face formidable challenges when attempting to verify a history of domestic violence, especially in the context of court proceedings. Because secrecy, denial, and cover-up are all integral threads in the fabric of violence, clinically validating a history of domestic violence requires sophisticated and sensitive interviewing skills, appropriate psychometric instruments, astute observation, and multiple sources of data. In some cases, verification of a history of abuse is not possible, because there are often few clues pointing to its existence. These cases are particularly disquieting to clinicians who are confident on an intuitive level but lack substantiating evidence to defend their case conceptualization and recommendations.

We are not suggesting that professional evaluators commence their work with the notion that every allegation of domestic violence raised during a child-custody dispute is valid. We are suggesting, however, that every allegation be taken seriously and followed up with a thorough and comprehensive investigation. Historically, domestic violence has been ignored, minimized, or denied and the family court system has not been a refuge for battered women and their children. Often, compelling data supporting a claim of domestic violence is overlooked or ignored by untrained professionals who are unable to see how one piece of information fits into an overall pattern of control and domination in an intimate relationship.

Within the context of a custody dispute, the tasks involved in assessing violence are twofold. The first task, and ultimately the most challenging, is to establish whether a history of domestic violence exists. Answers to questions about the severity, frequency, and duration of the violence must be unearthed. The second task is to examine the effect of the violence on the victims and their children. To accomplish these tasks, a variety of assessment tools must be utilized.

Many books, for example (Ackerman, 1995; Chisholm & MacNaughton, 1990; Leonoff & Montague, 1996; Stahl, 1994), address the issue of how to conduct custody and visitation assessments. These books offer important advice to legal and mental health professionals, as well as to divorcing parents, on the critical questions to be used in determining custody and visitation plans. The literature also details the relevant data and information that must be gathered to assist in answering these all-important questions. In addition to these resources, there are also important general guidelines on the ethical standards of practice for the professional groups that deal with the area of custody and visitation assessments (American Psychological Association, 1994).

Within these guidelines, there is general consensus regarding some fundamental principles as to how to properly conduct an assessment (American Psychological Association, 1994). For example, only properly qualified mental health professionals should conduct assessments; the purpose of an assessment is to recommend parenting arrangements in the best interests of the children; multiple methods of data collection must be utilized; assessments cannot be one-sided; the assessor must disclose any prior relationship between the clinician and any family members; evidence of child abuse or imminent harm must be reported to proper authorities; and the parents, whenever possible, should be empowered to develop a parenting plan that is in their children's best interest.

It is not the purpose of this book to repeat the contributions of others in how to conduct custody and visitation assessments. These works offer useful insights on the differing strategies and interventions required in high-conflict child-custody disputes. However, cases involving domestic violence require a comprehensive and coordinated community response well beyond the traditional response to divorcing parents by assessors and the family justice system (Jaffe, Lemon, Sandler, & Wolfe, 1996).

The specialized skills and knowledge base required by mental health professionals involved in custody dispute cases with domestic violence must be firmly rooted in an appreciation for the private nature of intimate violence. Many abused women do not report their victimization to law-enforcement professionals, child-custody evaluators, family law lawyers, or judges. In fact, in a large-scale study conducted in Canada, 22% of women reported that they did not disclose their abuse to anyone (Rodgers, 1994). Their secret was kept from their doctor, neighbors, closest friends, and family. Complicating this propensity for battered women not to reveal their victimization to professionals and supportive loved ones is the predictability that actual batterers will deny their abusive behavior. Children, as prisoners of their parents' custody war, are often reluctant to disclose what they heard or witnessed during the course of the marital relationship. As a consequence, multiple assessment strategies and sources of information must be employed.

The courts and mental health professionals face the same dilemma. In the face of scant evidence to evaluate the likelihood of a domestic violence history, clinicians must rely on interviews, questionnaires, direct observation, and multiple collateral sources. The utility of an assessment is heavily contingent on the nature of the information gathered during the assessment process. As discussed previously, custody disputes routinely involve allegations and counterallegations. Instead of throwing up one's arms and concluding that the matter is simply one of "he said, she said," a clinician must mine information and data from a variety of sources beyond the parents themselves. Possible sources of additional data that may shed light on the veracity of the competing allegations are the police, previous therapists, family doctors, school personnel, child protection workers, friends, neighbors, and family. These sources may all be invaluable quarries of information.

In our experience, evidence of a history of victimization can often be uncovered through small pieces of a larger puzzle. Because definitions of domestic violence refer to an overall pattern of behavior beyond individual acts of violence, court-related professionals need to access multiple sources of information. This can be problematic if the professionals who have been involved with the family lack the training and awareness to be able to identify warning signs. Obviously, proper training is required to ensure that the right questions are asked and clues are properly analyzed within a clear framework. The audience for our work cannot be limited to psychologists, psychiatrists, or social workers engaged in completing custody and visitation assessments. Our purpose is to inform the broad range of professionals, community members, and parents whose daily lives are touched by this issue.

❖ WHAT TO ASSESS

One of the most fundamental stumbling blocks to verifying abuse is the tendency of doctors, teachers, counselors, clergy, court-related professionals, and others to avoid directly asking victims if there has been a history of domestic violence. Increasingly, curriculum in various professional fields is addressing this issue. The unspoken mantra of "don't ask, don't tell" is giving way to the more informed position that domestic violence must be directly screened for within a cross-section of situations. Yet our experience is that when individuals are simply asked, "Have you been abused?" the resulting answer is commonly "no." The "no" can mean that the victim does not consider her experiences "abuse," or she may be uncomfortable acknowledging that she has been victimized for a variety of reasons. Empirical research has shown that when women are victimized, only 17% view their experience of spousal violence as a crime and only one third agree that their experience makes them a victim of "domestic violence" (Johnson & Bunge, 2001). To accurately screen for intimate violence, general questions should be avoided. Rather, specific and direct questions, such as "Have you ever been frightened by your ex-partner's temper?" or "Has your ex-partner ever controlled your ability to contact friends and family?" should be posed. The answers to these types of questions often prove enlightening.

Also of significance is the assessor's knowledge of the various manifestations of abuse, which can include physical abuse, sexual abuse, property violence, and psychological abuse (Walker, 1979). Assessors must have a clear understanding of the severity, frequency, and duration of these forms of violence. They need to understand who the perpetrator of the violence was; what effects the violence had on the victim and the children; what intervention services were employed; and what the likelihood is that the abuse will reoccur.

When assessing the effects of violence, it is important that court-appointed evaluators and judges not decontextualize the experiences of women and children. The line between what is considered adaptive versus maladaptive can be elusive. For example, a child who is behaving as a "child-management problem" within a classroom is likely to be viewed as suffering adjustment difficulties. However, the child's adjustment may, in fact, be praiseworthy when his or her home life is considered. Similarly, a battered woman who presents herself as "hostile" may be coping in an exemplary fashion, given her alternative options. A quiet, compliant student, who is superficially deemed to be behaving adaptively, may indeed be terrified of "misbehaving" as a consequence of witnessing her father's wrath. Without context, the determination of adjustment is hollow.

Outside observers must also appreciate that the effects of violence are not static. The victims of violence, as well as their children, cope with the aftermath within a cultural, societal, and individual context that is in a perpetual state of flux. Similarly, the manifestations of experiencing multiple forms of violence can have their own ebb and flow. The time period following separation can be a particularly challenging time for battered mothers and their children. This stressful time can trigger a state of crisis. A mother who has experienced abuse and is being threatened with the prospect of losing her children to her abuser may not manage her circumstances well. It is during this particularly difficult period when her parenting skills are scrutinized by the court and every flaw or mistake is magnified by her batterer.

Nature of the Abuse

Domestic violence comes in many forms, including physical, psychological, sexual, and economic abuse. At the core of domestic violence is the abuse of power and control. This concept is symbolized by the well-known Duluth, Minnesota, diagram (Figure 2.1) of a wheel with behavioral components in the spoke subsections. As the wheel highlights, the centerpiece of violence is power and control. The various elements of abuse are used to garner and maintain this control. Common tactics include coercion and threats, intimidation, isolation, blaming the victim, denial of abuse, and the exploitation of the children as weapons against the mother. Often these distinct strategies are utilized in concert with devastating consequences. Many battered women have remained captives in their homes because of their abusive partners' threats to pursue custody if the relationship ends. The Duluth model also captures the ways in which children are frequently used as a means of sustaining control and power.

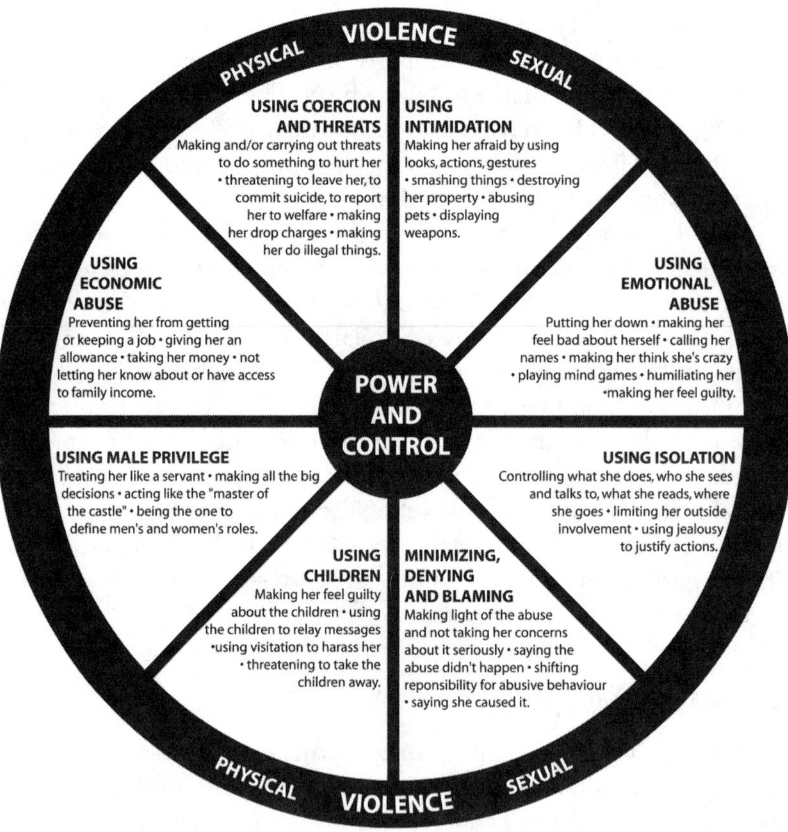

Figure 2.1. Power and Control Wheel
SOURCE: Developed by the Domestic Abuse Intervention Project, Duluth, MN.

There are several self-report questionnaires to assist in screening for domestic violence. Among the more well-known is the Conflict Tactics Scale (CTS; Straus, 1979), which has been used extensively in research. A revised version of this instrument has also been created (Straus, Hamby, Boney-McCoy, & Sugarman, 1996). Despite the widespread use of the CTS, it has been met with significant criticism. For example, the CTS has been criticized for not considering the consequences of violence, the context in which the violence occurs, and the full range of abusive behaviours (see Dobash, Dobash, Wilson, & Daly, 1992; Jouriles, McDonald, Norwood, & Ezell, 2001). Violence used as a means of self-defense is not distinguished from violence inflicted to maintain control and domination.

A more thorough and sensitive questionnaire is the Abuse Observation Checklist (ABOC; Dutton, 1992). With Dr. Dutton's permission, we, with the assistance of a colleague, Dr. Karen Scarth, have expanded this valuable tool to be more applicable within the context of custody disputes; it is found in the Appendix. Respondents are asked if they have either experienced or inflicted a wide range of specific acts of violence. In addition, they are also asked if any of their children were exposed to the violence; the most recent occurrence of the violence; and whether the violence occurred during the marital relationship, post-separation, or both. Given the alterations to the instrument, it lacks empirical validation, but remains a valuable self-report measure for initially screening for violence. It is an essential beginning point to ensure that all forms of abuse are screened for.

If screening interviews and associated instruments reveal concerns related to a history of domestic violence, more detailed information must be gathered through additional interviews with both partners, children, and collateral sources. Critical domestic violence incidents (the first, worst, and most recent) will need to be detailed by the victims to provide a sequence of events and consequences, putting the violence into a chronological and relational context. The alleged perpetrator needs to be afforded an opportunity to respond to the detailed incidents. Prior to this, the evaluator must determine whether such a discussion may compromise the safety of either the mother or the children. Throughout any court-related evaluations, the safety of the parties and the children must be given priority. The commonly faced challenge is that alleged batterers often deny being abusive and may instead raise competing allegations such as mutual violence, mental instability, self-defense, or outright deceitfulness. The evaluator needs to keep an open mind, entertaining several competing hypotheses while gathering more data.

Domestic violence occurs along a continuum from severe violence, which may be life-threatening, to less overt forms of violence, such as emotional and psychological abuse. We do not condone any form of violence. However, it is important for mental health professionals and the courts to be able to differentiate the range of domestic violence to provide measured responses and utilize appropriate resources. Without a more sophisticated analysis, a parent who is genuinely remorseful and who has taken responsibility for his or her behavior may be in danger of having all parental contact terminated. On the other hand, a parent who is an ongoing danger to his or her ex-spouse and children needs to be given a clear message from the court that any future visitation will be denied in order to recognize safety as the primary issue.

Well-known researcher Janet Johnston has advanced a typology of domestic violence. Her classification of domestic violence acknowledges that violence may vary according to severity, frequency, circumstances, and perpetrator. The typology includes the following categories, which are not mutually exclusive: Ongoing/Episodic Male Battering, Female Initiated Violence, Male Controlling Interactive Violence, Separation/Divorce Trauma, and Psychotic/Paranoid Reactions (Johnston & Campbell, 1993). Domestic violence advocates have been critical of Johnston's typology, suggesting that she fails to recognize the overwhelming role of gender inequality, power imbalance, and social injustice (Dalton, 1999). Other researchers and clinicians have been wary of such a typology because it minimizes the seriousness or consequences of violence that occurs at the time of separation, by implying that violence inflicted at that time is more situational and, therefore, not indicative of a pattern of abuse. Although that may be true, the magnitude of the trauma or fear on the part of women and children is not diminished by the fact that the violence occurred at separation. Additionally, Johnston's typology study suffers from a very small sample size, only about 100 families in total.

There is a broader concern that categorization of violence will be misused by male perpetrators of domestic violence to minimize their abusive behavior by blaming their victims or proclaiming that the abuse was uncharacteristic. However, as long as the proportion and impact of male violence is properly recognized and identified, attempts to classify types of battering will assist clinical practice and future research endeavors. Johnston has generated hypotheses about the differential impact of exposure to violence on boys and girls within these five categories. She also recognizes that there is overlap between the categories, which necessitates caution being exercised by those assessing domestic violence.

Meaning of Violence

As discussed previously, because many victimized women do not view themselves as having experienced domestic violence, they will respond "no" to the question "Have you been abused?" Concluding the assessment process at that point could have a potentially dangerous outcome. Time must be devoted to having mothers, fathers, and children describe what violence within the home means to them. Each person in the family may share memories of the same occurrence of violence, each with a unique intrapsychic meaning. For example, the father may describe "restraining" his wife "for her own protection," which should arouse concern. The mother may describe the event as the terrifying evening in which her husband put his hands around her throat. Child witnesses may report that their "mommy didn't do as she was told, making daddy mad." It is important for evaluators to delve into not only what was done, when, and by whom, but also the meaning and purpose of the violence.

In our clinical practice, we have interviewed women who experienced an incident of domestic violence several years ago. Although some court-related professionals may view this act as uncharacteristic and isolated and, therefore, irrelevant, a deeper exploration of the incident reveals its significance. These women often describe how from the moment of the assault their energies are absorbed by attempting to avert another attack. The event is a pivotal experience in the life of an abused woman. From that day forward, the potency of her husband's glare increases dramatically. He need not resort to violence to maintain his unilateral and omnipresent control. The ripple effect of that "isolated incident" reverberates throughout the marriage.

Lethal Violence

Clearly, within the context of custody disputes where there is a history of domestic violence and the batterer has recently lost his partner and fears losing his children, the assessment of lethality must be considered. Although assessors and judges must be prepared to entertain competing hypotheses about the existence of domestic violence, it is imperative that these cautions not jeopardize the safety and well-being of the victim and her children. In this regard, there must be heightened vigilance about the possibility of lethal violence.

There is a growing body of literature that suggests a cluster of common factors associated with domestic homicides and suicides (Hart, 1990; Campbell et al., 2001; Hassler, Johnson, Town, & Websdale, 2001; Quinsey, Harris, Rice, & Cormier, 1998). Initially, domestic violence advocates proposed that the following factors be given significant weight in assessing lethality: threats of homicide or suicide, fantasies of homicide or suicide, possession of weapons, a sense of ownership of the abused partner, centrality of the partner, impending or recent separation, escalation of risk taking on the part of the batterer, repeated law-enforcement involvement, and hostage-taking (Hart, 1990). Researchers have validated many of these factors and added consideration of the victim's perception of the perpetrator's capacity to inflict grave harm (Weisz, Tolman, & Saunders, 2000). Although this research is still in its infancy, it does provide important guidance for the police and other professionals in gathering data and attempting to determine the level of risk within a particular home. Obviously, predictions related to potential to commit lethal violence are far from precise. However, the majority of tragedies are preceded by significant warning signs that are ignored by various professionals and agencies (Office of the Chief Coroner, 1998, 2002).

❖ WHOM TO ASSESS

Victimized Mothers

Women may not be prepared to share their abusive experiences during a court-related evaluation. Some women may not be comfortable with the evaluator. They may fear being judged, not being believed, or feeling ashamed of all they endured—especially in the area of sexual victimization. They may weigh the benefits of disclosing such information against a host of potential costs imposed by their ex-partner. Other women may not label their experiences as abuse and rather accept them as the reality of intimate relationships or the natural cycle of any separation. More recently, many women have been instructed by their counsel not to raise issues related to domestic violence for fear that there may be court-imposed sanctions for not being a "friendly parent" or for being an "alienator."

The harsh reality for many women is that they are forced to choose between the lesser of two evils. If they attempt to fight for custody and behave in a protective manner toward their children, they risk being punished by the court system for being "unfriendly," "unreasonable," or "harmful" to their children. Alternatively, if they capitulate to the demands of their ex-partner, they perpetually fear for their children's safety. The question of which is the lesser of the two evils haunts many battered women.

Mothers who have experienced domestic violence may present themselves in an "off-putting" manner to lawyers, judges, and court-appointed evaluators. Some battered women may seem unstable, highly anxious, or angry. Other victimized women may present themselves with flat affect and a seeming indifference to their abuse history. The effects of trauma must be well understood by individuals working with battered mothers (Briere, 1997a; Dutton & Goodman, 1994; Jones, Hughes, & Unterstaller, 2001). Traumatic stress commonly results in psychic numbing or detachment, depression, guilt, and a poor self-image. For many battered women, the months and years of being isolated, degraded, threatened, and assaulted are akin to what is inflicted on prisoners of war. However, their prison guard is someone they love, someone they live with, and someone they have children with.

Tactics such as attempts to distort reality, forced psychological and financial dependence, threats of violence, and pursuit of custody are frequently utilized by batterers. The impact of these experiences can lead to profound changes in battered women. It is imperative that women who have experienced violence be evaluated within the context of this reality.

Elevations on psychological tests are not uncommon for both parents. Even when child-custody disputes do not involve a history of domestic violence, significant elevations on either a clinical scale or a validity scale are not unusual. These findings must be interpreted with great caution, within cases involving domestic violence as well as cases where domestic violence is not a concern. There is an inclination to either overinterpret or overweigh a significant elevation on a psychometric inventory. In cases involving domestic violence, the risks associated with relying too heavily on testing are particularly troubling. Batterers' response styles may hide problematic personality traits, whereas victimized mothers may score in the clinically significant range for depression, anxiety, PTSD, and somatic complaints. These findings, without an appreciation of the context, may lead evaluators to conclude that the battering father is better adjusted than the victimized mother. Battered mothers have been particularly disadvantaged by elevations on subscales related to "paranoia," despite the fact that their "paranoia" may be quite reasonable when their experiences of being stalked and harassed by their former partners are taken into consideration.

Battering Fathers

Batterers represent a heterogeneous population. There is no single psychological profile for a batterer. Some perpetrators of domestic violence conduct their reign of terror behind the closed doors of their home. Other perpetrators are violent whenever they feel a challenge to their perceived authority. Some men enjoy a "good" fight at the bar on a Saturday or in their homes (Healy, Smith, & O'Sullivan, 1998). Some batterers are most violent when they are drinking or abusing drugs. The alcohol and drug abuse problems of these perpetrators must also be addressed; there must be accountability in both areas. For a minority of batterers, the violence is associated with a serious mental disorder. In these circumstances, qualified mental health professionals must be available to monitor responses to medication as well as adjunct therapies where required. The problem of mentally disordered perpetrators is highlighted by a recent tragedy in Ontario in which the police, child-protection services, and a mental health center were unable to prevent a man with a severe mental health problem from killing his wife and four children (Office of the Chief Coroner, 2001).

In the context of custody or visitation disputes, some cases are more straightforward because of a criminal conviction. Even in these circumstances, however, one has to review all the court material as well as assessment and treatment records. The usual explanations that arise in these cases include the following: The violence was an isolated incident; the violence was not serious; the violence was serious but of a historical nature with little relevance to the present circumstances; and last, the violence was serious but limited to the spouse and, therefore, irrelevant because the children were not abused. This last argument was successfully presented by O. J. Simpson's legal team in his custody trial against the maternal grandparents, but was ultimately rejected by the California Court of Appeal.

In the aforementioned circumstances, it is important to find out the initial facts of the case that may have been "downsized" as part of a plea bargain in criminal court. Although there are cases that represent isolated incidents totally out of character for the spouse, convictions most often represent the culmination of a pattern of behavior. Research suggests that there are multiple and serious incidents of violence before the police get called and prosecutors proceed with charges (Jaffe et al., 1996). Interviews with the victim and perpetrators are essential starting points to uncover the history of violence.

In custody disputes, judges and lawyers often throw up their hands in despair and commonly state that it is a case of "he said, she said." When allegations are diametrically opposed, legal professionals are often undecided as to who to believe. Custody evaluations must review allegations with each party and give each side an opportunity to explain what happened. It may be helpful to have the alleged perpetrator complete a standard inventory about the abuse (ABOC), to engage him in a discussion about what transpired during the course of the relationship. Important considerations in the interviews include acknowledgment of violence, remorse over violent behavior, understanding the effect of violent behavior on spouse and children, commitment to change, and willingness to enter a batterers' intervention program.

Some men deny their violence in an honest and genuine manner, which raises the possibility that the allegation is false, or that the violence was initiated by their partner. Other men will deny being violent and use euphemistic terms such as needing to "restrain" their partners. When allegations are valid, most cases demonstrate a clear pattern of bullying or controlling behavior where individual acts of violence and abuse are designed to dominate or humiliate the partner. An analysis is required of these patterns, their intent, and the impact on the victims.

Often overlooked is the array of emotional and psychological abuse tactics designed to maintain control over a spouse without leaving physical marks. This abuse is easy to minimize and blends into the background of an unhappy and highly conflicted marriage. The Duluth Power and Control Wheel is a good tool to discuss the actual abusive behaviors and their effect.

At the extreme end of the continuum of violence are batterers who are dangerous and perhaps even lethal to their partners and children. In these circumstances, a risk-assessment inventory should be utilized. Although less than 1% of battered women are killed by their partner, they are in greatest danger at the point of separation. Fatality reviews in several states, such as Florida, as well as research in this area, suggest a number of lethality "red flags." These include prior history of domestic violence, obsessive possessiveness and morbid jealousy, threat to kill, the perpetrator's perception that he has been betrayed by his partner, prior police calls to the residence, drug and alcohol abuse, possession of an injunction, and prior criminal histories of victims and perpetrators (Hassler et al., 2001). Although the predictive validity of these "red flags" has not been thoroughly tested, the concept of risk assessment is important in a number of ways. The "red flags" offer service providers in different sectors a common language, an awareness that domestic violence can be lethal, and feedback for victims who need to discuss the implications for safety planning (Hassler et al., 2001).

In child-custody disputes, several factors have been highlighted in addition to the aforementioned "red flags." These factors include specific threats to harm the children or an extended fantasy of murder/suicide of the family. Another factor is threats to abduct the children to ensure that the spouse will never see them again. In cases where the batterer has citizenship in a foreign country, this threat is of particular concern.

In some cases, it may be appropriate to consider interviewing former partners of alleged batterers. Former partners, unlike current partners, are more likely to provide evaluators with an accurate account of the level and nature of violence within the previous relationship. Sometimes, however, former partners may refuse to be interviewed because they continue to fear the batterer or may have children with the batterer.

War-Torn Children

It is estimated that in the United States alone, between 3.3 and 10 million children witness violence in their home annually (Davidson, 1994). It is now clearly documented that children exposed to domestic violence are at risk for a range of emotional and behavioral difficulties. Many still believe that in order to be affected children must directly observe the infliction of violence. While many children are exposed to this level of horror, many others are deeply affected by more indirect exposure. For example, children may hide under their beds or in their closets while listening to objects being smashed, blows to their mother, or pleas from their mother (to their father) to stop. These children, although not directly witnessing their mother's assault, may nonetheless fear she will be injured or killed. Children in these circumstances do not react in a uniform fashion. Whereas some may fear for their mother's safety, others may be angry with their mother for not leaving. Some children may experience divided loyalties, whereas still others may be overwrought with guilt regarding their inability to intervene and protect their mother. Professionals who interview and observe these children must be aware of the experiential differences among children exposed to domestic violence.

The most common measure used to evaluate children's adjustment both in research and clinical practice is the Child Behavior Checklist (CBCL; Achenbach & Edelbrock, 1983). Within the context of a custody dispute, typically both parents are asked to complete the inventory and the child's teacher is asked to complete a modified version. Although this measure provides an overall picture of how a child is doing across a number of areas, it does not specifically address the issue of children's exposure to domestic violence.

More recently, efforts have been made to specifically address this gap. For example, Grych, Seid, and Fincham (1992) have developed the Children's Perception of Interparental Conflict Scale; Singer and Song (1995) have developed an Exposure to Violence Scale; and Graham-Bermann (1996) has developed the Family Worries Scale. These scales, in combination with the more standard CBCL measure, can provide court-appointed evaluators with significant data as to the nature of adjustment difficulties and the exposure to conflict.

There have also been recent developments in measuring the level and severity of trauma-associated symptomatology. For example,

Briere (1976b) developed the Trauma Symptom Checklist for Children; Wolfe developed the Children's Impact of Traumatic Events Scale (Wolfe, Gentile, Michienzi, Sas, & Wolfe, 1991); and Ruggiero and McLeer (2000) empirically examined the PTSD scale of the Child Behavior Checklist. Just as it is important to assess for trauma-related symptomatology in battered mothers, similarly it is important to evaluate children for trauma-specific difficulties. (For an in-depth review, see Geffner et al., 2000; Kerig, Fedorowicz, Brown, & Warren, 1998.)

As highlighted in Chapter 1, children of divorce are at risk of suffering long-term adjustment difficulties. For children exposed to domestic violence, both during the marital relationship and following separation, the obstacles to healthy adjustment are much more formidable. Research on children exposed to domestic violence has shown that children's difficulties can vary greatly by age and stage of development. Table 2.1 highlights the range of problems that research has shown can arise from exposure to domestic violence. As is evident in the table, children can be affected by their experiences quite differently, even siblings exposed to the same level and severity of violence. There is no single presentation or profile of a child exposed to domestic violence.

❖ DIFFERENTIAL APPROACHES

The interventions, resources, and appropriate outcomes are not uniform from one custody case to another. Families come in many forms and the solutions to family breakdowns must take into consideration the unique needs and challenges of a particular family. Child-custody cases involving domestic violence demand tailored legal and mental health interventions. By way of simple analogy, a basic toolbox contains nails, screws, and fasteners, as well as a hammer, screwdriver, and wrench. The choice of tool depends on the hardware appropriate to complete the task. Similarly, within the "toolbox" of judges, lawyers, and various mental health professionals, an array of "tools" or interventions exist; each must be used under specific circumstances. To use a hammer on a screw may, indeed, work, but not well and at potentially great costs. Cases involving domestic violence are fundamentally different from cases wherein domestic violence is not an issue and, thus, the remedies, be they legal or otherwise, need to be distinctive.

Table 2.1 Impact of Exposure to Domestic Violence

Infants	*Preschool Children*	*Latency Elementary School (5–12 Years)*	*Early Adolescence (12–14 Years)*	*Later Adolescence (15–18 Years)*
Failure to thrive	Aggressive acts	Bullying	Dating violence	Dating violence
Listlessness	Clinging	General Aggression	Bullying	Alcohol/drug abuse
Disruption in eating and sleeping routines	Anxiety	Depression	Poor self-esteem	Running away from home
Developmental delays	Cruelty to animals	Anxiety	Suicide	Sudden decline in school achievement and attendance
	Destruction of property	Withdrawal	PTSD symptoms	Disrespect for females; sex-role stereotyped beliefs
	PTSD symptoms	PTSD symptoms	Truancy	
		Oppositional behavior	Somatic concerns	
		Destruction of property	Disrespect for females; sex-role stereotyped beliefs	
		Poor school achievement		
		Disrespect for females; sex-role stereotyped beliefs		

SOURCE: Reproduced with permission from Sudermann and Jaffe (1999), *A Handbook for Health and Social Service Providers and Educators on Children Exposed to Woman Abuse/Family Violence.* Ottawa, ON: Minister of Public Works and Government Services Canada.

The differential approaches required for child-custody disputes with and without domestic violence allegations are summarized in Table 2.2. We developed this chart in consultation with the Family Violence Prevention Fund (Jaffe, 1995) to assist in the training of lawyers and judges involved in custody proceedings. The major headings in the chart indicate the various levels of analyses involved in consideration of custody disputes.

Table 2.2 Differential Approaches to Custody Disputes

Issue	*Normal Visitation Dispute*	*Visitation Dispute With Allegations of Violence*
Central issue	Promoting children's relationship with visiting parent	Safety for mother and children
Focus of court hearing	Reducing hostilities	Assessing lethal nature of violence
Planning for future	Visitation schedule that meets needs of children	Consider no (suspended) visitation or supervised visitation
Assessment issues	Children's stage of development, needs, preferences Parents' abilities	Impact of violence on mother and children Father's level of responsibility Mother's safety plan
Resources required	Mediation services Divorce counseling for parents and children Independent assessment/ evaluation	Specialized services with knowledge about domestic violence Supervised visitation center Coordination of court and community services Well-informed lawyers

SOURCE: Adapted with permission from Jaffe (1995), *Children of Domestic Violence: Special Challenges in Custody and Visitation Dispute Resolution*. San Francisco, CA: Family Violence Prevention Fund.

❖ CONTROVERSIAL ISSUES

Is Parent Alienation Syndrome Real?

Although Parent Alienation Syndrome (PAS) has not been recognized by any major mental health or legal association, it has infiltrated the family justice system (Kerr & Jaffe, 1998). Richard Gardner, author of *The Parent Alienation Syndrome* (1992), posits that within the context of custody disputes, one parent either willfully or unconsciously attempts to alienate the child from the other parent. According to

Gardner, in the vast majority of cases the mother is the alienator and the father is the victim of her campaign. Gardner's unsubstantiated theory has been raised in a number of custody disputes in which the children express a desire not to see their father. His proposed remedy in extreme cases of Parent Alienation Syndrome is to transfer custody to the "victim" of the alienation and jail the alienator. The consequences of this theory's growing popularity and uncritical acceptance are particularly serious for victims of domestic violence. In these cases, a myriad of factors can cause the mother to exhibit the constellation of behaviors identified by Gardner. For example, children who have witnessed their mother's abuse may fear seeing the father post-separation. A mother's desire to protect her children from possible physical or sexual abuse may be viewed as alienating behavior. Critics of Gardner's theory point out that Parent Alienation Syndrome is not validated by any empirical studies, Gardner's work is self-published and not subject to peer review, and Gardner's theory is grounded in gender bias with its claim that 90% of alienators are mothers. (For a detailed analysis, see Dallam, 1999; Kerr & Jaffe, 1998.)

Ultimately, legal and mental health professionals face difficult challenges in situations in which children express a preference not to see one of their parents. Careful and thorough exploration as to why a particular child holds this view must be undertaken. Currently, there is a proclivity toward snap judgements and simplistic interpretations as to why a child is apprehensive about seeing a parent, and mothers are blamed when their children resist visitation. Other, more reasoned hypotheses about the genesis of a child's reluctance, such as having witnessed their father hurting their mother, appear anemic in the face of a competing allegation of Parent Alienation Syndrome.

Recently, Parent Alienation Syndrome has been reformulated to shift the focus to the alienated child. An alienated child is one who persistently voices unreasonable negative feelings and beliefs toward a parent that do not reflect the child's actual experiences with that parent. Although this line of inquiry is in its infancy, several theorists have postulated that alienation is best viewed as a fracture in the attachment between parent and child. Within such a framework, strong attachment would be at one end of the continuum and alienation would be at the other. In cases where the child does not appear to have a strong attachment to a parent, the salient question becomes "To what can this be attributed?" Possible explanations include a preferred affinity for one parent, an alignment with one parent, an estrangement from one parent as a result of past abuse, or alienation as a result of one parent's efforts.

In addition to Parent Alienation Syndrome, batterers are raising other counterallegations, such as Fictitious Disorder by Proxy, Munchausen by Proxy, and Malicious Mother Syndrome, as a means to deflect judicial attention from the allegations of domestic violence. The strategy of alleging that the victim is psychologically impaired can have a profound influence on how a custody dispute is addressed by court-appointed evaluators and judges. Systematic and thorough analysis must be conducted when allegations of violence and alienation coexist.

How Common Is Mutual Abuse?

Most social science research on the incidence of domestic violence, based on police reports and victim surveys, suggests that women are much more likely to be victims of serious violence. Nevertheless, the concept of "mutual violence" is gaining ground. Sometimes police officers have used the term when they cannot identify a clear victim and perpetrator and both parties have visible scratches or bruises. Some lawyers and judges may abandon any meaningful inquiry into the nature of the domestic violence and conclude that both parents are assaultive and, therefore, the violence is "mutual." There are few studies that have clearly defined or qualified mutual violence. One study on separated parents undergoing custody evaluations suggested that only 9% of couples fit this description (Jaffe & Austin, 1995).

Over the past decade, police departments have begun to fine-tune their arrest policies to account for the fact that a significant minority of the incidents to which they respond involve the use of violence by both parties. Examination of these cases shows that the use of violence by women can differ dramatically from that of men. For example, many women use violence against their abusers in attempts to protect themselves from their attackers. Mutual arrests were becoming common in many jurisdictions and the results are proving very problematic. First, children of battered women are being placed in foster care even though their mothers have histories of strong parenting and loving, supportive relationships with their children. Second, battered women are refraining from seeking police protection because they fear that they, themselves, might end up being arrested. Third, charges against the most violent and dangerous abusers are routinely dropped because their victims are also defendants.

As a result of these unfortunate and dangerous developments, which many characterize as unintended consequences of the use of the criminal justice system to stop battering, police departments are increasingly training their officers to investigate such cases for self-defense and to refrain from arresting the party whose use of violence was legitimate in the eyes of the law. Furthermore, police are being asked to investigate which party, if either, is the primary aggressor and to avoid arresting both parties where one is clearly more dangerous, more controlling in the incident, and more in need of government intervention to reduce the risk of serious harm to others in the family. Some states' statutes and many police departments' policies now include requirements that police avoid arresting both parties where one acted in legitimate self-defense or was the secondary aggressor and less dangerous of the two parties. This evolution of the role of law enforcement serves to reorient police to the primary purpose of police intervention in domestic violence cases and also serves to place the focus of intervention efforts where they are needed most critically (Frederick, 2001).

Do Children of Batterers Wish to Be in Their Primary Care?

In homes where there is domestic violence, children most often continue to love both parents. They may have confused and ambivalent feelings. They may love their mother and want to protect her. They often wish she would do more to protect herself. They may be frightened by their father's anger and threatening behavior. Children also may admire their father and forgive his outbursts by blaming alcohol, job stresses, or their mother. In short, there is no consistent interpretation of the violence and many conflicting emotions are raised.

Not surprisingly, many children, especially boys who identify with their fathers, may express wishes to live with him or choose him as a custodial parent. In some cases, the children have seen their mother emotionally and physically beaten down so much that they hold their father's view of her limited worth and no longer respect her as a parent. The challenge for judges, children's lawyers, and custody evaluators is to reconcile children's wishes to be with a batterer and their best interests. Only recently have researchers focused their attention on children's relationships with their mother's abuser. This preliminary research has found that children were more emotionally affected by an abusive biological father than by a stepfather. For these children, their biological fathers were the most emotionally available, although they reported lower self-competency compared with youths whose mothers' abusers were not their father figures (Sullivan, Juras, & Bybee, 2000).

The challenge in these circumstances is analogous to a situation in which a teenage daughter wants to live with her sexually abusive father because "he needs her." No court would accept this proposal. Nor should they accept a child's desire to live with an abusive parent. Children need to have safe visitation with a parent who is abusive, as long as that parent is involved in a treatment or intervention program and has accepted responsibility for the violence. However, visitation must be recognized and addressed as part of an overall plan for family members, rather than a child's right. Children's wishes must be placed in the context of their best interests.

Unfortunately, frustrating the wishes of older children and adolescents can cause them to run away or become totally unmanageable for the custodial mother. These are challenges that require multiple service providers and a coordinated plan of action monitored by the court.

Are Battered Women Poor Mothers?

Historically, it was thought that battered women suffered from some sort of major psychopathology. It is now generally accepted that the psychological profiles of battered women and nonbattered women are not different until the point at which battered women are assaulted. That is, many abused women suffer from trauma symptoms related to the experience of violence rather than problems inherent in themselves. What remains a contentious issue among academics and advocates is the extent to which being subjected to domestic violence has a detrimental impact on mothering, both in the short term and the long term. There are those who theorize that domestic violence fundamentally undermines a woman's capacity to parent. Others suggest that women's efforts to resist the violence, shield their children from the effects of abuse, and effectively parent are largely ignored in the literature (Radford & Hester, 2001). More recently, new research has empirically explored the effect of domestic violence on mothering

(Levendosky & Graham-Bermann, 2000; Levendosky, Lynch, & Graham-Bermann, 2000; Sullivan, Nguyen, Allen, Bybee, & Juras, 2000). Although this research is still in its infancy, critical issues related to mothering and domestic violence are being examined with findings that suggest most abused women make their children's well-being a priority. In the context of custody assessments, it is important for the assessors to be aware of abused women's parenting ability after the violence stops or before it began rather than blaming victims for the distress of living with violence. In any event, stereotyping abused women as inadequate mothers is misleading (Sullivan, Nguyen, et al., 2000).

Can Batterers Change?

The question of the likelihood of violent men changing is a critical one. Some judges appear overly confident that violent men can transform into good fathers by attending an anger-management group. Their confidence is such that some judges are inclined to award generous access on the assumption that change is an inevitable outcome of participation in a treatment intervention, such as anger-management or alcohol-abuse intervention programs. This optimism is simplistic and, in some cases, dangerous.

The transformation process for battering men in treatment is not straightforward. Among the more important variables are program integrity, program completion, genuine desire to cease being violent, and taking responsibility for the violence. Programs aimed at alcohol dependency will not transform violent men into nonviolent partners. The more appropriate intervention is a program geared specifically toward abusers. These programs are fairly widespread in the United States, Canada, New Zealand, and Australia. The typical model lasts anywhere from 20 weeks to a year. The aim of many programs is related to developing self-awareness, challenging attitudes and beliefs, acquiring new skills, and monitoring progress.

Increasingly, researchers have turned their attention to what programs or program elements work with which battering men. Despite some promising results (Dobash, Dobash, Cavanagh, & Lewis, 2000), the most daunting obstacle to successful intervention remains attrition. The problem of battering men either failing to start or failing to complete battering interventions plagues numerous programs. Most batterers do not enter into treatment programs with a desire to change their abusive behavior. More typically, violent men agree to ongoing participation to serve a more instrumental purpose. For example, a batterer may participate in a batterers' program in an attempt to keep his partner from leaving him, or to influence the courts to be more lenient in sentencing. Clearly, such ulterior motives do not reflect positively on the likelihood for change. Within the context of child-custody disputes, batterers may be even less likely to actively seek intervention or to take responsibility for their violent history. Counteralleging alienation is a far easier route.

For batterers who take responsibility, seek appropriate treatment, and demonstrate a history of noncontrolling and nonabusive behavior, admissions of violence should not be used to eliminate contact with their children. Recent reviews of the literature suggest that some programs show modest success especially if they are part of an integrated community response to domestic violence (Healy et al., 1998). In our own experience, batterers' intervention programs seem most hopeful for first-time offenders who have neither deeply rooted antisocial attitudes nor a problem with violence against women.

Aren't Most Allegations False?

A common charge of fathers' rights advocates is that women, in large numbers, falsely allege domestic violence and/or child abuse as a tactical move in family proceedings. Although the basic premise of this book is that domestic violence has been largely ignored by the divorce literature and the family court system, we need to be reminded that the concept of domestic violence can be misused by lawyers in their advocacy for their clients. It is appropriate for thoughtful judges to be concerned about domestic violence allegations raised as a legal strategy rather than genuine pleadings before the court, but they should never draw conclusions without a more in-depth analysis of what has actually transpired within the family.

Lawyers, judges, and evaluators must be vigilant to the possibility of false allegations. However, this alertness must not blind them to the prospect that the allegations are true. The options for genuine batterers are limited. They can either acknowledge their violence or deny the abuse and claim they are the victims of false allegations. Other less utilized options include counteralleging that the mother is mentally ill or delusional, or that she, in fact, was the aggressor. In assessing each allegation, one has to be reminded that the most common problem in this area is that domestic violence tends to be underreported rather than fabricated or exaggerated.

❖ CONCLUSION

Family court judges, lawyers, assessors, arbitrators, and guardians ad litem are confronted on a daily basis with competing versions of history within custody disputes. Through training and education, some of these professionals are aware that different approaches and interventions are required when custody disputes involve domestic violence. With regularity, mothers who have tangible evidence of domestic violence are forced into the "cooperative coparenting" cookie-cutter approach to resolving custody disputes. For some, the relevance of domestic violence is enigmatic. Words such as "shared parenting," "equal care time," "joint custody," and "coparenting" have become synonymous with the best interests of children; insufficient attention is paid to how the perpetration of violence is germane to parenting. Often, these professionals are blinded by the charm, friendliness, and approachability of the batterer. In our view, the presence of domestic violence requires a very different analysis of the custody dispute, unique assessment strategies, and differential court interventions. In the next chapter, we examine how courts around the world are now beginning to recognize this problem in their legislation and decision making by the family courts.

3

Changing Legislation and Legal Practice to Recognize Domestic Violence in Child-Custody Proceedings

As stated in the first chapter, domestic violence does not end with the separation of the spouses. In fact, it may increase after separation, when the batterer realizes that he is losing control of his partner. Often the batterer uses the legal system to continue the abuse, fighting for sole or joint custody or extensive visitation in order to continue to control the former partner and the children. One California child-custody researcher found that her assistants could always identify which court files involved domestic violence; those files were significantly thicker than the nonabuse files, indicating that the parties had undergone much more litigation. Similarly, a formerly battered woman in Berkeley, California, told one of the authors that her ex-partner had dragged her into court 42 times in the previous year, arguing over custody and visitation issues. Her stress-related disability and the mental health of the children became much worse as a result until the court finally put a stop to this abusive and expensive behavior.

Batterers may also fight hard to keep their former partners and their children from relocating. This can keep the former partner isolated from family and friends, unable to pursue an education or a new job, and unable to follow a new spouse who has been offered higher educational opportunities or better employment in another location. It can also keep the former partner under the surveillance of the batterer, replicating the dynamics of the original relationship.

Legislatures in many states, provinces, and countries are starting to recognize these problems and address them through laws specifying that domestic violence is an important factor in custody and visitation decisions. However, we do not see the same awareness when it comes to relocation issues. Most jurisdictions make this process difficult, if not impossible, if the "left-behind parent" objects; exceptions are not made for domestic violence cases. Although the Hague Convention on the Civil Aspects of International Child Abduction provides some protections in cases where a battered parent flees with a child to another country to avoid the abuse, the standard that the "taking parent" must meet is a very high one. Additionally, some states, provinces, and countries have yet to even address domestic violence as a custody factor in their statutes.

❖ INTERNATIONAL TREATIES

The first international treaty dealing with child custody was the Hague Convention on the Civil Aspects of International Child Abduction, which was opened for signature in 1980. As of April 2000, 65 countries had signed it, including the United States, Canada, New Zealand, and Australia. The convention's provisions are available to citizens of the signing countries when one parent moves with a child under 16 years of age to another of the signing countries over the objections of the other parent. Although the preferred response is to order the child's swift return to the home country, there is an exception if "there is a grave risk that his or her return would expose the child to physical or psychological harm or otherwise place the child in an intolerable situation." This exception has sometimes been interpreted to include domestic violence cases, as will be discussed in Chapter 4.

A later convention, the Hague Convention on the Protection of Minors, was adopted in 1996, but is not yet in force. It has not been signed or ratified by any of the four countries discussed in this book, though this may happen in the next few years. This convention establishes international standards for the exercise of custody jurisdiction and the enforcement of custody orders. It includes recognition of orders made by contracting states, and makes special provision for situations in which "urgent measures" are called for—which could presumably include domestic violence. Because this convention is not yet operative, references to the Hague Convention in this book refer to the 1980 Convention on Child Abduction.

❖ UNITED STATES LAWS

Several policy statements by national groups in the United States have addressed domestic violence as a custody factor. Since the U.S. legal system excludes family law cases from the federal courts (with the exception of international law when Hague Convention cases may be brought in either federal or state court), there are no federal laws addressing this issue. However, as indicated in Chapter 1, the U.S. Congress has spoken on this topic in an advisory capacity. U.S. Congressional Resolution Number 172, authored by Representative Constance Morella and passed unanimously in 1990, states in part: "It is the sense of Congress that, for purposes of determining child custody, credible evidence of physical abuse of a spouse should create a statutory presumption that it is detrimental to the child to be placed in the custody of the abusive spouse."

The National Council of Juvenile and Family Court Judges created a national taskforce composed of domestic violence experts, judges, prosecutors, defense attorneys, and legislators, which worked for three years on a Model Code on Domestic and Family Violence, unveiled in 1994. Section 401 of this Model Code states a similar policy: "In every proceeding where there is at issue a dispute as to the custody of a child, a determination by the court that domestic or family violence has occurred raises a rebuttable presumption that it is detrimental to the child and not in the best interest of the child to be placed in sole custody, joint legal custody, or joint physical custody with the perpetrator of family violence." This section is intended to apply not only to protection order cases but also to all divorce, delinquency, and child-protection cases (National Council of Juvenile and Family Court Judges, 1994).

Section 404 of the Model Code puts forth a similar policy with regard to modifying custody orders, after the initial decision has been made: "In every proceeding in which there is at issue the modification of an order for custody or visitation of a child, the finding that domestic or family violence has occurred since the last custody determination constitutes a finding of a change of circumstances." This is important because it sets "a change of circumstances" as the standard for modifying a pre-existing custody order. In states that adopt this Model Code, such as Maine, a custody order may be changed when domestic violence occurs after the court has issued the order.

Along the same lines, the American Bar Association (ABA) adopted a resolution and model statute in 1989 that states: "Joint custody is inappropriate in cases in which spouse abuse, child abuse, or parental kidnapping is likely to occur." An ABA report also recommended that states adopt legislation establishing a presumption against custody to batterers (Davidson, 1994). The ABA report also urged that domestic violence against a parent be used as a defense to allegations of abandonment, thus removing such allegations from consideration by the custody judges, in cases in which a battered parent fled for self-protection and left the children behind.

The Uniform Child Custody Jurisdiction and Enforcement Act (UCCJEA), replacing the Uniform Child Custody Jurisdiction Act and enacted in 14 states as of late 1999, includes provisions for emergency jurisdiction in a new state if the parent and child fled to that state to escape from abuse. It also states that the petitioning parent does not have to disclose to the other parent the child's residential addresses for the last 5 years if there has been partner or child abuse. And it also states that courts cannot use the fact that a parent unilaterally took the children while escaping from abuse as grounds for refusing to hear a case based on interstate flight by a parent fleeing from domestic violence (Zorza, 1999).

The National Council of Juvenile and Family Court Judges issued a 1990 report, *Family Violence: Improving Court Practice*, in which it recommended that courts weigh and consider violent conduct in making custody and visitation orders; recognize that there may be an unequal balance of power or bargaining capability between the parties, which requires a more careful review of the custody and financial agreement before approval by the court; and not presume that joint custody is in the best interest of the children. The report further recommended that if there is a recent history of violence, offenders should be ordered to successfully complete treatment specifically for the violence, and for substance abuse if necessary, before custody or unsupervised visitation is awarded (National Council of Juvenile and Family Court Judges, 1990).

In summary, many nationally recognized bodies in the United States have spoken out about the importance of taking domestic violence into account when custody and visitation decisions are made. These statements emphasize the effects on children of living in homes where abuse is taking place, as well as the significant overlap between partner abuse and physical or emotional abuse of children.

Custody

Over the last several decades, the standard that U.S. courts were directed to apply in custody cases, "the best interests of the child," has been relatively vague. Recently, however, two distinct and opposing trends have served to clarify this standard. The first trend, starting in the late 1970s, incorporates a preference for joint custody in most cases (e.g., Tennessee statute). This type of legislation is usually initiated by fathers' rights groups and opposed by domestic violence advocates. The other trend, which is also supported by much social science data as described in Chapter 2, has increasingly supported limits on custody rights for domestic violence perpetrators.

By the end of 2000, 47 U.S. states, plus Washington, D.C., and Puerto Rico had passed laws addressing custody and visitation decisions in which domestic violence had occurred (Elrod & Spector, 2001; to check current code sections, see the National Council of Juvenile and Family Court Judges database at www.dvlawsearch.com/pubs/). In most states, these laws either specifically allow courts to take domestic violence into account when making custody decisions, or actually mandate that they do so. The latter approach is recommended by the Model Code on Domestic and Family Violence, section 402(1). Of course, even with statutes specifying that courts must take domestic violence into account, such laws do not clarify what weight should be given to this evidence. Consequently, courts have been known to allow the evidence to be presented, but have seemingly ignored it in their decisions, as will be discussed in Chapter 4. As of September 2001, 17 U.S. states plus the District of Columbia had gone further by creating a "rebuttable presumption." Their law states that once domestic violence has been proven by the battered partner, the burden shifts to the perpetrator to prove why it is in the best interest of the child to be with him or her. For example, Louisiana law states that sole custody is to be given to the parent who is less likely to continue family violence.

In these states, statutes may still vary greatly in terms of what evidence is considered sufficient to trigger the presumption. The most stringent requirement is found in states such as Florida and Delaware, which require a conviction for domestic violence before the presumption is triggered, thus requiring proof beyond a reasonable doubt in the criminal case. Similarly, some states, such as Idaho, have legislation authorizing courts to terminate parental rights when one parent is convicted of murdering or intentionally killing the other. The next most stringent standard is the "clear and convincing evidence" standard in such states as Oklahoma. Some states, such as Wisconsin, require evidence of a crime of domestic violence, though not an actual conviction. At least one state, Louisiana, requires either "serious bodily injury" or at least two incidents of domestic violence. Some states require a "history of domestic abuse" (Iowa) or "ongoing domestic abuse" (Oklahoma) to trigger the presumption. The lowest standard for actions resulting in a presumption against a perpetrator of domestic violence in a custody case is "credible evidence" of domestic violence (North Dakota) or simply "evidence of domestic violence" (Minnesota). Note that this abuse may not amount to criminal activity, depending on the state's definition of domestic violence.

Similarly, state statutes vary as to what evidence is needed to rebut the presumption once it is triggered. For example, Pennsylvania requires proof that the batterer has successfully completed a batterer's treatment program if he or she has been convicted of certain crimes. Delaware and California require proof that there have been no further acts of domestic violence, that the perpetrator has completed a batterer's treatment program and any drug or alcohol program ordered by the court, and that the court order (which gives joint or sole custody to the batterer) would be in the best interests of the child. North Dakota requires that there be clear and convincing evidence that the best interests of the child require the abusive parent's participation as a custodial parent.

Wisconsin, which has a presumption against joint custody in domestic violence cases, requires clear and convincing evidence that the perpetrator will not interfere with the abused partner's ability to cooperate in future decision making before the presumption can be overcome. Louisiana requires successful completion of a batterers' treatment program, refraining from abuse of alcohol or illegal drugs, and demonstrating that the absence or incapacity of the abused parent or other circumstances are such that custody granted to the perpetrator is in the best interests of the child.

State laws may also require courts to articulate their reasons for awarding sole or joint custody to batterers. This reduces the number of cases in which courts "split the difference," awarding joint custody where they are unable to truly determine which parent should have custody, and minimizing evidence of domestic violence. It also cuts down on some judges' practice of automatically awarding joint custody except in the most egregious cases. Finally, requiring courts to state their reasons on the record makes it easier to appeal the decision, as the appellate court can examine the stated reasons and compare these to the evidence presented at a hearing or trial. Thus, the reviewing court can better determine whether the decision was so inappropriate as to be an abuse of discretion. Although it is rare that appellate courts overturn custody decisions, there are instances where this occurs, as discussed in Chapter 4.

Other state laws require specific judicial findings of fact that the custody or visitation arrangement best protects the child and victim from further harm (e.g., North Dakota). In New Hampshire, Montana, and Ohio, when judges order joint custody in the face of a history of domestic violence, they must make findings of fact that joint custody is not detrimental to the child, despite the violent history.

A few statutes give specific direction about custodial awards when a parent is charged with or convicted of certain violent or sexual crimes. For example, Pennsylvania law states that in these cases, the court must appoint a qualified professional to provide specialized counselling and must take testimony from this professional prior to awarding custody or visitation to the convicted parent. The Pennsylvania law also states that if custody or visitation is awarded to that parent, the court may require subsequent periodic counselling and reports, and may modify the award if there is a threat of harm to the child. Similarly, Arizona statutes allow custody or visitation to be suspended when a parent is charged with certain crimes against children, even before the parent is convicted.

In some cases, it may appear that both partners have been violent toward each other. Louisiana's statutes address this by excluding self-defense or defense of a child or another family member from the definition of domestic violence, and by allowing a determination of which partner was the primary aggressor. This is an important provision, as battered partners frequently fight back. South Carolina and Nevada also have primary aggressor language in their custody statutes. Language used in some of the aforementioned presumption statutes, such as "history of abuse," "pattern of abuse," or "ongoing domestic abuse" helps ensure that an isolated instance, where the battered partner became physical in self-defense, does not carry the same weight as repeated abuse by the other partner.

Some statutes specify that domestic violence is a defense against charges of abandonment by the abused parent, who may have fled the family home without the children in order to protect herself or himself (e.g., Colorado, Iowa, Kentucky, Maine, South Carolina, and Florida). The language used in many of these statutes indicates that it probably came from Section 402(2) of the Model Code on Domestic and Family Violence. Domestic violence may also be a statutory defense to concealing the child, if the battered parent takes the child with her or him when fleeing (e.g., California and Michigan).

At times, the statutes requiring courts to take domestic violence into account conflict with other statutes that give preference in custody decisions to the parent most likely to allow or encourage "frequent and continuing contact" with the other parent. These are usually referred to as "friendly parent provisions," and are based on the assumption that the "friendly parent" is a better parent because she or he is fostering the relationship between the child and the other parent.

These provisions can work against an abused parent, because the batterer may appear in court to be a more "friendly" parent. The abused parent often wants to limit contact with the batterer, which may appear to judges, mediators, evaluators, and other court staff as hostility—when, in fact, it may be due to fear about her or his own safety and the safety of the children. Some legislatures have specifically addressed this dilemma, stating that if there is a conflict between ordering frequent and continuing contact on the one hand, and prioritizing the child's safety on the other, concerns about the child's health, safety, and welfare should prevail (e.g., Oregon, California, Iowa, and Maine). Providing for frequent and continuing contact between the child and both parents becomes a secondary priority in such cases. Minnesota's custody law specifically states that the determination of which parent is the more friendly should not apply in custody cases where there is a history of domestic violence.

Several of these statutes appear to be based on the Model Code on Domestic and Family Violence, Section 402(1)(a), which states that the court shall consider as primary the safety and well-being of the child and battered parent. Similarly, Florida and California have enacted policy language stating that perpetration of domestic violence in a home where children reside is detrimental to children. These provisions maintain the best interests of the child as the paramount goal.

Battered parents may sometimes be seen as unstable and unable to protect the children from the batterer, even after separation. In addition to the custody arena in Family Court, this situation may lead to criminal charges of "failure to protect," or may arise in juvenile court, where the battered parent's parental rights may be terminated. In Iowa, Minnesota, and Oklahoma, laws have been passed stating that domestic violence is a defense to such an allegation. This is also seen in an ABA policy statement: "Laws should be carefully crafted to provide for an affirmative defense to a civil or criminal charge of parental failure to protect a child from abuse. That defense should address situations where accused parents had a reasonable apprehension that acting to stop or prevent the child maltreatment would result in substantial bodily harm, to themselves or to their children" (Davidson, 1994, p. 18). Unfortunately, when battered women are charged with failure to protect their children from batterers, it is all too possible that they will be criminally convicted of this crime and/or lose custody of their children as a result. This is discussed in Chapter 4.

State Laws on Visitation

Legislation in the area of visitation has shown the same shift in awareness, with many U.S. states now specifying that parents who have perpetrated domestic abuse be treated differently than nonviolent parents. Barbara Hart, a prominent domestic violence legal commentator, summarized U.S. state laws on visitation in domestic violence cases: "Collectively, the codes appear to create a new legal principle: To wit, the existence of domestic violence in a family militates against an award of unsupervised visitation to the abusive parent" (Hart, 1992). At their mildest, these laws require courts to consider awarding supervised visitation once a restraining order has been issued, so that the abusive parent is not alone with the child (e.g., California). A stronger version of this is found in statutes establishing a rebuttable presumption against unsupervised visitation with a batterer (North Dakota and Oklahoma). Or the statute may require the court to order supervised visitation once domestic violence has been proven.

For example, Louisiana, which has the strictest laws on this topic, requires that a batterer's treatment program be completed before the supervised visitation commences. Additionally, the perpetrator must not be abusing drugs or alcohol, must pose no danger to the child, and visitation must be found to be in the child's best interests. The Louisiana statute also states that the supervised visitation must not be overnight or in the home of the perpetrator; the supervisor cannot be a friend, relative, or associate of the violent parent; and the violent parent must pay the costs of supervision.

States are also starting to pass laws restricting or terminating visitation when one parent has been convicted of killing the other parent (e.g., Massachusetts). If a parent is convicted of first degree murder of the other parent, some states bar visitation with any of the couple's children, unless such visitation is specifically found to be in their best interest (Nevada, Massachusetts, and California). Presumably, courts in states without such statutes would also have the power to deny visitation if they found that such contact was contrary to the best interest of the child.

Many states have laws regulating the providers of supervised visitation, creating standards which they must meet, establishing clearinghouses for locating such programs, or funding such centers (see, e.g., Florida, Hawaii, Kansas, and California, and Section 406 of the Model Code on Domestic and Family Violence). Other laws state that the visitation order must be very specific as to the time, place, and manner of transfer of the child (e.g., California). This limits the chances of further abuse taking place during the exchanges. It also cuts down on any reason for the parents needing to communicate with each other to clarify an unclear order. This change came about because visitation orders frequently used to provide for "reasonable visitation," which was a recipe for disaster in many families, because it allowed the abusive parent to interpret this vague term in almost any way he or she wished. Batterers who pounded on the door at midnight demanding to see their children were sometimes not arrested for violating the restraining order or for disturbing the peace, because police were not sure if this fell within the realm of "reasonable visitation."

Some states call on the court to protect the child and/or the abused parent from further harm when crafting visitation awards (e.g., Vermont, New Jersey, and Illinois). In Arizona, Florida, Kentucky, Missouri, Minnesota, New Hampshire, Rhode Island, Washington, and California, the court is authorized by statute to deny visitation to an abusive parent when limits on visitation, such as supervision, are inadequate to protect a child from abuse, abduction, or other harm.

South Carolina passed legislation that adopted the visitation section of the Model Code on Domestic and Family Violence (Section 405). This section states that visitation is prohibited unless the court finds that adequate protection can be provided to the child and victim. For example, the court may order an exchange of a child to occur in a protected setting, or order supervised visitation. (See Chapter 5 for expanded discussion of supervised visitation and potential court conditions.)

The South Carolina statute goes on to state that the judge may, on her or his own motion, limit or bar visitation to provide for the child or victim's safety and order the address of the child or parent to be kept confidential. The provision for the judge to act on his or her own motion is important, in that a significant percentage of family law litigants have no attorneys. The South Carolina law also states that the court may order the perpetrator to pay the costs of any medical or psychological treatment of a child who is injured as a result of one or more acts of domestic violence.

In at least one state, New Jersey, the statute provides that the court must consider any request by the plaintiff for an investigation or evaluation to assess the risk of harm to the child before the visitation order is made. And many statutes state that visitation shall not be ordered before a hearing is conducted to determine the best interests of the child. Some state statutes provide that any visitation order can be modified if the noncustodial parent threatens or harms the child, consistent with Section 404 of the Model Code on Domestic and Family Violence (e.g., Arizona, New Jersey, and Minnesota). Of course, judges in states without such statutes may also modify orders in such situations, if they find this to be an example of "changed circumstances."

Sometimes third parties, such as grandparents, petition the court for visitation. A few states have laws requiring the court in such cases to consider whether either parent has been convicted of domestic violence (e.g., Ohio). State laws may also mandate that the court investigate any friction between the grandparent and the custodial parent and look at the circumstances surrounding the demise of the nuclear family (New Hampshire). In other words, if domestic violence was the reason for the breakup, and the batterer's parents are now seeking visitation over the battered party's wishes, in some states the court must take this into account in determining what is in the best interests of the children. Ideally, all family law judges would consider these factors, even without a statute explicitly requiring them to do so. However, see the case decided by the U.S. Supreme Court in 2000, discussed in Chapter 4, *Troxel v. Granville.*

State Laws on Adoption

Vermont has a statute that provides for termination of the birth father's rights if he is a batterer. Montana requires that domestic violence be considered as a factor in determining whether to approve adoptions. Maryland statutes state that if a parent has been convicted of domestic violence against the other parent, this shall be considered in determining whether to allow an adoption without the perpetrator's consent. And Colorado and New York mandate criminal domestic violence background checks for people applying to become adoptive or foster parents.

State Laws on Relocation

Relocation is an especially important issue for battered women. As mentioned earlier, many batterers try to keep their former partners from moving to a new area as part of the ongoing attempt to control the ex-partner and children. Unfortunately, statutes in the United States often force battered women to stay in close physical proximity to the batterer in order to facilitate visitation, due to policies favoring "frequent and continuing contact."

The Model Code on Domestic and Family Violence incorporates a presumption that the custodial parent should be allowed to relocate with the child if this parent decides that relocation is in the child's best interests (Section 403). Tennessee has adopted a milder provision, requiring that when the court is ruling on a relocation request, it must consider evidence of physical or emotional abuse to the child, the other parent, or any other person. However, Janet Bowermaster, a leading commentator on relocation and domestic violence, points out that even the Model Code does not go far enough in terms of protection for battered women and their children who need to flee the area. The shortcoming is that no provision exists for cases in which the parent realizes, before a custody order is issued, that sudden flight is necessary for protection (Bowermaster et al., 1998). Under current law in most states, such flight may be seen as child abduction by the battered parent, and may result in a criminal conviction and loss of custody. Ironically, if the battered parent does not take immediate steps to protect the child, she or he may be seen as having "failed to protect" the child. The parent may be caught in a "catch-22" situation, where either way he is seen as acting wrongfully. The Violence Against Women Act, in recognition of the need for instant protection for a fleeing victim of abuse, wisely provides that every state must give full faith and credit to the orders of protection issued by every other state. However, it does not grant such protection for custody orders that are granted by other provisions of federal and state law.

Statutes need to be adopted throughout the United States providing that, in domestic violence cases, sudden flight may be appropriate to protect children and battered parents from further abuse. California has adopted such legislation, providing a defense to criminal child-abduction charges if the parent or child has been subjected to mistreatment or abuse. It requires the taking parent to file a custody action and notify the prosecutor in the home county of the child's current location. The statute also mandates that the prosecutor keep the location information confidential from the battering parent.

Other statutes also provide models of what victims of domestic violence need in order to build new, violence-free lives. Along these lines, Ohio's statute states that even though the custodial parent must notify the court of any intended relocation, if one parent is convicted of battering the other, the court may not disclose the desire to relocate to the batterer, unless such notice is in the best interests of the child and is supported by the court's specific written findings of fact.

Some states, such as Maine, consider domestic violence a factor in restricting the perpetrator's access to children's records (school, medical, etc.). This is particularly useful if the battered parent is attempting to relocate. Other states protect the confidentiality of the abused parent's address, so the abuser cannot locate the victim, as recommended in Section 405(3) of the Model Code. The Violence Against Women Act, a federal statute, requires the U.S. Postal Service to promulgate regulations to secure the confidentiality of domestic violence shelters and the abused person's (or abused people's) address.

Several states have adopted Address Confidentiality Programs, administered by the Secretary of State's office (e.g., Washington, Rhode Island, Illinois, Nevada, and California). These statutes provide that a relocating victim of domestic violence and her or his children can keep their new address confidential from the general public and the other parent. Although this type of law does not affect existing custody or visitation orders, it can help prevent the perpetrator's stalking and reinjuring the victim and children. Pick-up and drop-off of the children in such cases would, of course, occur at a location other than the victim's home, and would ideally be done by a neutral third party to prevent further abuse to the battered parent.

Similarly, statutes need to address cases in which abused parents move after a custody and visitation order has been issued. Although courts strongly prefer that such parents file a motion to modify the original order before moving, this is not always possible in terms of protecting the child or the abused parent. The aforementioned California statute appears to provide a defense in such situations, and should be widely adopted. South Carolina also directs the court to disregard any relocation of a parent against whom an act of domestic violence has been perpetrated, if that parent was not the primary aggressor. Iowa and Arkansas have similar statutes. Statutes in some of these states appear to be based on the Model Code, Section 402(2).

Professor Bowermaster recommends speeding up court cases in which one parent requests permission to move, so that the other parent does not win through financial attrition. When cases take a long time to resolve, the poorer parent (often the mother) may lose the case simply because she can no longer afford an attorney. Further, the longer the abuser has access to her, the more opportunities he has to harass and stalk her at work, often causing her to lose her job. Minnesota has adopted a statute similar to the Model Code provision, stating that the custodial parent may move unless the other parent shows that the move is not in the best interests of the child, or is sought to interfere with visitation. A unique aspect of this legislation is that a court hearing is not required unless the noncustodial parent meets a basic "threshold" standard of proof regarding one of the (previously mentioned) two points in his or her pleadings. This system is much less expensive for the parties. It also is much less likely to result in the courts unwittingly participating in the noncustodial parent's ongoing attempt to control and abuse the custodial parent (Bowermaster, 1998).

State Laws Regarding Mediation of Custody and Visitation Disputes

Another important area of law concerning custody and visitation disputes in which domestic violence is a factor is court-ordered mediation. In many U.S. states, courts are empowered or required to send all custody and visitation disputes to court-connected mediators. In some of these states (Minnesota, North Dakota, Oregon, Maine, Washington, Louisiana, and Pennsylvania), all cases involving domestic violence are exempted from mediation. In others, parties are allowed to opt out of mediation, due to concerns about the inherent power imbalance between the parties and the consequent dangers to the battered partner from mediating with the batterer (New Hampshire and Ohio). In Indiana and California, joint parental counseling may also be prohibited in domestic violence cases. An additional reason why domestic violence cases may be exempted from mediation is that mediators may not be able to obtain accurate information if one of the parties is so afraid of the other party that she (or he) cannot speak freely to the mediator. (See also Sections 408(A) and 408(B) of the Model Code, providing two alternatives for states, one prohibiting mediation when a restraining order is in effect, and one allowing mediation—but with safeguards.)

In other states, although victims of domestic violence may be ordered to go to mediation, there may be provisions for the parties to be seen separately at the battered partner's request, or to bring a support person into the mediation session with the battered partner, as described in Section 407 of the Model Code (see, e.g., California and Tennessee). The support person is usually not allowed to participate or give advice, but is present for moral support.

Training about domestic violence is increasingly mandated for professionals dealing with victims and children. At least one state, California, has legislation requiring all child-custody evaluators to undergo domestic violence training, both initially and during annual updates. Many states also require child-custody mediators to undergo domestic violence training, and to screen for domestic violence, as recommended in Section 407 of the Model Code (see, e.g., Hawaii,

California, Oregon, and Tennessee). Minnesota has mandated judicial training on the subject of domestic violence and child custody. Statutes in various states also require domestic violence training for child-protection workers, social service workers, school personnel, attorneys appointed by the court to represent children, doctors, nurses, and mental health professionals. Some states also incorporate into their mandatory batterer-education programs a unit on the effects of domestic violence on children (e.g., Washington). These are valuable provisions, which should be universally adopted (Astor, 1994).

❖ NEW ZEALAND

As in the United States, laws in New Zealand historically treated domestic violence as irrelevant to custody and access (visitation) decisions. The Guardianship Act, which governs custody and access, was silent about domestic violence as a factor. Until July 1996, the sole factor in such cases was the vague "best interests of the child" standard. Given the traditional attitudes of courts, this resulted in many cases in which abusers were either awarded custody or very liberal access.

In 1990, Professors Ruth Busch and Neville Robertson were commissioned by the New Zealand Victims Task Force to study repeated breaches of protection orders. This study included interviews with many battered women, judges, family court counselors, police officers, shelter workers, and attorneys. It also included reviews of many cases, both reported and unreported. The recommendations covered all aspects of domestic violence laws, including requiring judges to consider the effects of being exposed to violence when determining the best interest of the child. The recommendations also stated that joint custody was inappropriate when violence had characterized the spousal relationship. Further, they stated that access to the abusive parent should be supervised or denied if the child's or primary caregiver's physical or emotional health would be endangered by unsupervised visitation.

The 300-page report, with 101 recommendations, was so heavily edited by the government before publication that the authors withdrew their names from it in protest. However, when the public became aware of this censorship, more attention was paid to the original report and its recommendations, mobilizing support for changes.

In this climate, three children were killed in 1994 by their custodial father, a batterer who then committed suicide, an all-too-common scenario in domestic violence cases. In an *ex parte* order (i.e., the mother had not been notified), the father had been given custody 3 months earlier, in spite of a former protection order and a pending protection order for the mother. These deaths galvanized the country, with the former chief justice of New Zealand issuing a report to the minister of justice in which he criticized the court's decision to give the father custody and recommended that the Guardianship Act be amended. Specifically, the former chief justice advised the adoption of a rebuttable presumption against custody or unsupervised visitation to spouse abusers and child abusers. This presumption could be rebutted only by convincing the court that the child would be safe with the violent parent. The presumption appears to be modeled on the U.S. Model Code on Domestic and Family Violence (Busch & Robertson, 2000).

The following year, the Domestic Violence Act 1995 was adopted, as were amendments to the Guardianship Act, the Family Proceedings Act, and the Legal Services Act. These changes were very large, incorporating a power and control analysis of domestic violence into the statutes. The definition of domestic violence in the Domestic Violence Act is very broad, incorporating not only physical abuse but also sexual abuse, psychological abuse, and other tactics commonly used by perpetrators. The legislation also specifies that acts which "when viewed in isolation can appear to be minor or trivial" may form "part of a pattern of behaviour" against which a victim can claim protection. Additionally, while the Act defines psychological abuse as including, causing, or allowing a child to watch physical, sexual, or psychological abuse of a family member, it also clarifies that "the person who suffers the abuse is not regarded as having allowed the child to see or hear the abuse." This is essential to protect battered parents from charges of "failing to protect" their children from the batterer. The responsibility rests squarely on the batterer for exposing children to this behavior.

The amendments to the Guardianship Act incorporate concerns about violence escalating at the point of separation, during access (visitation) changeovers. Section 16B(4) includes the aforementioned recommendation from the former chief justice: The Family Court shall not make any order giving custody or unsupervised access to a party who has used violence against the child who is the subject of the proceedings, a child of the family, or against the other party unless the court is satisfied that the child will be safe with the violent party. In determining this safety issue, the Act lists several criteria:

- The nature and seriousness of the child and/or spousal violence
- How recently and frequently such violence has occurred
- The likelihood of further violence
- The physical and emotional harm caused to the child by the violence
- The opinions of the other party as to safety of the child
- The wishes of the child (depending on his/her age and maturity)
- Steps taken by the violent party to prevent further violence from occurring

Further, Section 15(2B)(b) of the Guardianship Act mandates that the court consider imposing "any conditions for the purpose of protecting the safety of that other parent while the right of access conferred by the order is being exercised (including while the child is being collected from, or returned to, that other parent)." These are important provisions in terms of recognizing the need for continued or increased protection for the child and the abused parent after the parties have separated, and are helpful in clarifying what "best interests of the child" means in domestic violence cases. Protecting the custodial parent is essential in itself, and is also a key component in providing for the best interests of the child.

The effects of these statutory changes in terms of case decisions will be discussed in the next chapter.

❖ CANADA

Federal Legislation

Canadian statutes first acknowledged domestic violence in divorces in 1968, when physical and mental cruelty became grounds for dissolution of marriage. Currently, Canadian laws, both federal and provincial, require custody and access (visitation) disputes to be decided based on the child's best interest. As previously discussed, this standard is vague, and leaves a great deal up to the discretion of each judge, based on the facts of each case. Additionally, federal legislation states that parents are presumed equally entitled to custody of their children. This is another hurdle for victims of domestic violence to overcome if they fear the consequences of contact between the child and the abusive parent. Joint custody is also allowed, though not preferred, in Section 16(4) of the Divorce Act, with no mention of whether a joint custody order is appropriate in domestic violence cases.

Once custody has been determined, laws in Canada state that courts should grant the noncustodial parent maximum contact with the child. This policy may conflict with other policies, such as the parental duty to protect children from harm, which is required by provincial child welfare legislation. Failure to protect a child may result in the child's being found to be a "child in need of protection," which is grounds for removal of the child from the parent's custody.

Another troubling statute is Section 16(10) of the federal Divorce Act, which contains a "friendly parent" provision similar to that found in many U.S. states, providing that once a custody determination has been made, the court shall "give effect to the principle that a child of the marriage should have as much contact with each spouse as is consistent with the best interests of the child and, for that purpose, shall take into consideration the willingness of the person for whom custody is sought to facilitate such contact." This provision completely ignores the existence of domestic violence and child abuse in many families, and assumes that contact with each parent is necessarily in the best interests of the child—which in many cases is not the case. Additionally, as Professor Nicholas Bala notes, "[t]he tone of s.16(10) . . . may sometimes make those seeking custody reluctant to put forward a claim to restrict access for fear of appearing 'unfriendly.' This is unfortunate, as access can be very problematic in a relationship where there is an abusive spouse" (Bala, 2000).

But probably the most problematic provision in national legislation in terms of domestic violence and custody or access is found in Section 16(9) of the Divorce Act: "In making an order under this section, the court shall not take into consideration the past conduct of any person unless the conduct is relevant to the ability of that person to act as a parent of a child." Similar language is found in the Ontario Children's Law Reform Act, Section 24(3). As will be discussed in more detail in the following chapter, this language has sometimes been interpreted by judges as excluding all evidence of domestic violence at the hearing or trial. This language leaves up to each judge the determination of whether domestic violence is relevant to parenting ability—with consequently unpredictable results.

Fortunately, judicial education programs in Canada have dealt with domestic violence since the early 1990s, and have included presentations by advocates for battered women and their children. These programs seem to be having a positive effect on judicial awareness of the impact of domestic violence on children, as recent Canadian judicial decisions reflect an increasing emphasis on domestic violence in custody cases. These will be discussed in Chapter 4. Another promising development is the inclusion of domestic violence as a defense to parental kidnapping, if the child is taken to protect him or her from a danger of imminent harm. This is found in the Criminal Code, Section 285.

The 1998 release of a Parliamentary report, *For the Sake of the Children: Report of the Special Joint Committee on Child Custody and Access*, is also a positive step. Recommendation 16.11 states that any "proven history of family violence" should be a factor in any best interests decision regarding custody or access. It urges that Canadian laws be amended to this effect. Commentators have expressed concerns about inclusion of the term "proven" in the recommendation, because this appears to reflect an unwarranted fear of false allegations. This issue was raised by fathers' rights groups who heckled battered women while they were testifying at the hearings, as discussed previously (Bala, 1999). Obviously, no court would consider domestic violence unless it could be proven. However, the overall recommendation is a significant step forward.

Canada should seriously consider adopting a presumption against custody to batterers in the federal Divorce Act, which could be rebutted only by specifically enumerated actions, such as successful completion of a lengthy batterers' treatment program with no further incidents. Other useful presumptions suggested by leading Canadian commentators include joint custody being seen as inappropriate in cases where domestic violence has occurred, and a presumption against access in cases involving postseparation assaults. As Grace Kerr, one of these commentators, has noted, "Such reforms are necessary because the current laws in Canada not only require the abused spouse to prove that the domestic violence occurred, but also to prove that same is relevant to the 'best interests' determination" (Kerr, 1998).

Provincial Legislation

Child-protection statutes in Alberta, New Brunswick, Nova Scotia, Newfoundland, Saskatchewan, and Prince Edward Island specifically refer to domestic violence as a factor in finding that a child is in need of protection. Although this may be indicative of increased awareness of the importance of protecting children from domestic violence, such statutes can also be applied in ways that penalize battered women for "failing to protect" the children from the abuser. This will be explored in Chapter 4.

Additionally, some Canadian child-welfare legislation requires "any person" who has reasonable and probable grounds to believe that a child is in need of protection to report the situation (see, e.g., Ontario's legislation); clearly, "any person" would include the parents of the child. Thus, arguably, all parents who are themselves victims of domestic violence are legislatively mandated to report to the authorities the fact that their children are in danger. These laws pose serious problems for battered mothers, who may have their children removed if they comply with this mandate to report (Echlin & Osthoff, 2000).

Surprisingly, there is no legislation in Canada, federal or provincial, which specifically addresses domestic violence as a custody or access factor, except in Newfoundland. This statute, c.-13, Section 31, states: "The merits of an application under this Part in respect of custody of or access to a child shall be determined on the basis of the best interests of the child." And further: "In assessing a person's ability to act as a parent, the court shall consider whether the person has ever acted in a violent manner towards (a) his or her spouse or child; (b) his or her parent; or (c) another member of the household, otherwise a person's past conduct shall only be considered if the court thinks it is relevant to the person's ability to act as a parent."

Ontario passed a similar law in 1989, the Children's Law Reform Act. Recent amendments in Ontario require consideration of domestic violence in custody cases, and provide that access may be denied if the person reasonably believed the child might suffer physical or emotional harm. However, these reforms have not yet been proclaimed in force, nor is there a likelihood that they will be.

It is recommended that other provinces adopt similar legislation, to clarify that domestic violence by one parent against another is a key element of the best interests of the child standard.

Recent statutes in Alberta, Ontario, Saskatchewan, and Prince Edward Island providing for protection orders are starting to address the issue of custody and access in domestic violence cases. For example, the legislative history of the Alberta statute indicates that the drafters carefully considered danger to children in domestic violence cases, and attempted to craft language best designed to protect both children and their custodial parents from further abuse. They also closely examined the interaction between federal and provincial protection orders involving custody and access, and discussed the need for a presumption against custody to the abusive parent during the term of the temporary protection order. A leading Canadian commentator notes, "The Ontario legislation specifies that a restraining order under it takes precedence to any order for access (or custody) and allows for a variation of custody or access orders, reflecting a concern that protection of safety takes priority over a parent's right to contact with a child. The Alberta, Prince Edward Island, and Saskatchewan statutes specify that the court should consider the best interests of the child along with other factors in making a domestic violence order, which also implies that an order under these domestic violence statutes takes precedence to custody or access orders" (Bala, 2001, p. 16).

Another promising new development is found in Ontario's Domestic Violence Protection Act 2000, which allows courts to order a batterer into counseling as a condition of having court-ordered access.

It is recommended that all Canadian jurisdictions enact statutes such as Newfoundland's, to specifically acknowledge the significance of domestic violence for child-related proceedings. Also needed are better enforcement of existing laws and orders, including restraining orders; increasing support services for victims and their children; programs for abusers; and facilities to supervise access (Bala, 2001).

❖ AUSTRALIA

Like laws in most countries, until recently Australian legislation did not consider one parent's abuse of the other parent relevant to determining fitness as a parent. The Federal Family Law Act 1975 adopted the vague "welfare of the child" standard, which in practice incorporated consideration of child abuse, but not adult abuse, in custody and access decisions.

In 1989, the United Kingdom passed a new custody law, the Children's Act 1989, which took effect at the beginning of 1992. This law emphasized the need for both parents to share equally in decision making with children and stressed the need for children to have ongoing contact with both parents after they separated. Notably, the Children's Act 1989 did not provide for any exceptions in domestic violence cases.

The Australian Parliament took note of this new UK law, and formed a Joint Select Committee to review Australian national law on this topic; the Committee's report was released in 1992. The Committee was lobbied heavily by fathers' rights groups, who pushed for legislation that they felt was more father-friendly, in spite of studies showing that, in fact, courts did not appear to show gender bias in awarding custody and that most parents already felt that they should continue to be involved in their children's lives after divorce. There were no studies showing a need for legislative changes, and only anecdotal evidence as to the positive effects of the new UK statute. (This anecdotal evidence included many cases in which battered mothers and their children were pressured to remain in contact with abusive fathers and not allowed to relocate farther away from them.) Although the Committee's recommendations, which urged more shared parental responsibility and contact, were not implemented right away, they were reflected in the changes that took place in 1995 (Graycar, 1995).

In 1993, the Australian Law Reform Commission took up the issue of family law. By this time, the National Women's Justice Coalition had formed and lobbied for any changes to reflect the danger to children and mothers in domestic violence cases. The Commission issued a report in 1994, *Equality Before the Law: Justice for Women*. The report was based on over 600 oral and written submissions, including many statements by women about the effects of violence on their lives and the failure of the legal system to respond to this abuse. The Commission and several women's groups called for amendments to the Family Law Act to acknowledge both the deleterious effects on children of witnessing spousal abuse, and the significant overlap between partner abuse and child abuse. Additionally, the Commission recommended that the Equality Act should recognize that violence is an integral part of the inequality of women in Australia. Meanwhile, yet another group, the Family Law Council, was also examining Australian legislation concerning parenting. It released reports in 1992 and 1994 urging the adoption of legislation paralleling the UK Children's Act 1989.

These multiple calls for change resulted in the Family Law Reform Act 1995 (effective June 1996), repealing Part VII of the old Family Law Act, and replacing the "welfare of the child" standard with the "best interests of the child" standard. The most significant change is the new concept of shared parental responsibility. This means that responsibility for children is to be shared by parents irrespective of their separation (Section 61C(2)) unless the court makes a specific order stating that only one parent will make decisions about the child (Section 61D). Before this change, a parent who received sole custody retained all or most legal authority, although courts were already authorized under the Family Law Act to issue joint physical and legal custody orders.

The Reform Act contains major internal tensions, reflecting the conflicting goals of both the fathers' rights groups and the feminist groups. For example, Section 60B(2)(b) sets forth, among other principles, "the child's right to know and be cared for by both parents" and "the child's right of contact, on a regular basis, with both parents." However, Section 68F(2) of the new legislation states that the matters the court must take into account in determining the best interest of the child include "the need to protect the child from physical or psychological harm caused, or that may be caused by: being subjected or exposed to abuse, ill-treatment, violence or other behaviour; or being present while a third person is subjected or exposed to abuse, ill-treatment, violence or other behaviour" and "any family violence involving the child or a member of the child's family."

Similarly, Section 68K states that the court must ensure that the parenting order does not expose a person to "an unacceptable risk of family violence," and Section 43 of Part 4A adds to the list of principles "the need to ensure safety from family violence." Furthermore, attorneys are required to bring to the attention of the Family Court any existing family violence orders. The failure of the Reform Act to give specific guidance to courts in resolving this fundamental conflict between contact with both parents on the one hand, and protection in domestic violence cases on the other, is a major problem, as will be discussed in Chapter 4.

Although it does not use the term "joint custody," the Act introduces for the first time the concept of joint parental responsibility, which has already proven to be problematic in domestic violence situations in the United States. Shared responsibility or joint custody can give batterers, who are already focused on their own rights rather than on the needs of people around them, more control over their children and former partners. Similarly, "custody" and "access" orders are now called "residence" and "contact" orders—to reflect the new emphasis on shared parenting; the child's primary residence with one parent no longer automatically gives that parent the right to make decisions about the child without first consulting the other parent.

The *Act* also provides for "specific issues" orders, through which the court can make orders specifying how particular issues regarding the children are to be dealt with (i.e., exceptions to the general "shared decision making" rule). A leading Australian commentator noted that such orders can be a double-edged sword: Although they can provide for more flexibility, they also "sometimes allow the non-resident parent to assert a degree of control over the resident parent that is not mirrored in the actual distribution of caring responsibilities" (Dewar & Parker, 1999).

Other amendments in the Family Law Reform Act deal with the relationship between residence and contact orders issued by the federal Family Court and the domestic violence orders made by various state courts. Division 11 of the Act specifies that if the Family Court issues an order inconsistent with an existing domestic violence order, it must explain why it has done so and have someone explain the situation to the parties in language they can understand, including

- The purpose of the order
- The obligations under the order
- The consequences of a breach of the order
- The reasons for departing from the family violence order
- How the order may be varied or discharged
- The order must specify how any contact provided for in the order is to take place

These provisions seem useful for the other countries discussed in this book to incorporate, because as in many cases, there are conflicting orders and the parties do not know which order is in effect or how to reconcile the orders. And specificity in orders regarding residence and contact where domestic violence has taken place is crucial to avert further violence.

The Family Law Reform Act further provides that when issuing domestic violence orders, state courts may modify or overrule an existing residence or contact order issued by the Family Court, if this is in the best interests of the child. (However, apparently the usual practice is for judges to state that the domestic violence order is being issued subject to any existing contact order, or to direct the parties to return to Family Court to modify the contact order.) A national registry of court orders, accessible to all the judges, is necessary to better provide for this coordination, and is being developed in Australia; other countries and states are also creating such registries.

A further problem with the Act is that it encourages mediation in residence and contact cases, and lacks clarity as to whether domestic violence cases are exempted from this process. On the one hand, one commentator states that Order 25A of the Act, which preceded the Reform statute, prohibits mediation in domestic violence cases or cases in which there is any concern about the safety of the parties or their emotional, psychological, or physical health. On the other, another commentator states that both the Act itself and the chief justice's Direction as to the "Management of Cases Involving Family Violence" are ambiguous, leaving up to the discretion of the judge whether mediation should take place (Behrens, 1996). As previously mentioned, the use of mediation in domestic violence cases in the United States has been found to be problematic. Unfortunately, this emphasis on private agreements in the Reform Act may counteract many of the gains that might be expected from the explicit inclusion of family violence in the legislation.

Additionally, until Family Law Act restraining orders are enforceable by police, as recommended by the Law Reform Commission, they will remain largely ineffective.

As will be discussed in Chapter 4, initial reports of practice under the Reform Act paint a troubling picture for adult and child victims of domestic violence dealing with family law matters in Australia. There is an urgent need for further amendments to prioritize the safety of adult and child victims of domestic violence as more important than the child's right to stay in contact with both parents, when there is a conflict between these two policies. Additionally, given that the Reform Act will no doubt lead to the denial of many requests for relocation by victims of domestic violence and many orders requiring ongoing contact with the abusive parent, enactment of legislation providing for a national Confidential Address Program might be helpful in protecting the new secret addresses of victims of domestic violence and their children.

❖ CONCLUSION

In the United States, New Zealand, and Australia, there has been a great deal of recent progress in the area of legislation addressing the interface between domestic violence and custody decisions. Most states in the United States now either allow or require judges to take domestic violence into account in making custody decisions. Similar laws have recently been passed in New Zealand and Australia. Laws in the United States and New Zealand are also starting to address the need for specific visitation orders, the inappropriateness of mediation in domestic violence cases, the need for batterers to undergo treatment for this behavior before they have unsupervised contact with their children, and other important issues. Similar legislation is developing in Canada and reported cases are indicating judges' increasing awareness and sensitivity to domestic violence.

However, the work of passing laws addressing this important topic has really just begun. There is a need for additional legislation, including legislative guidance for judges as to how to reconcile apparently conflicting mandates from the legislature. These mandates often take the form of encouraging frequent and continuing contact with both parents on the one hand, while protecting children from abusive parents on the other. Additionally, statutes need to clarify what should happen when a formerly battered parent wishes to relocate to a new area, away from the batterer, with or without a custody order, and to give due weight to the history of abuse in making such a determination. Many of the new statutes mentioned in this chapter and the Model Code on Domestic and Family Violence provide useful guidance for future legislative efforts.

Further, passing laws is only the first step. Equally important is the implementation and interpretation of the legislation. Chapter 4 addresses this issue, and also considers how judicial decisions may reflect an awareness of domestic violence, even in the absence of legislation requiring that it be taken into account.

4

From Theory to Practice

The Varying Responses of the Court System to Domestic Violence in Child-Custody Cases

Two prominent U.S. researchers noted that, in their study, dissolution cases involving violence toward women were significantly more likely to include custody disputes (Liss & Stahly, 1993). The American Psychological Association reported that abusive fathers were at least twice as likely to dispute custody as nonabusive men (American Psychological Association, 1996; Liss & Stahly, 1993).

Recent court decisions in child-custody disputes show a trend toward recognizing the importance of domestic violence as a factor. Even in states or provinces without statutes requiring that domestic violence be considered, increasingly courts are not only considering a history of domestic violence but also, at times, giving it significant weight in their decisions. However, there are still large numbers of cases in which judges, especially trial judges, appear not to comprehend the relevance of partner abuse when making custody or visitation decisions.

Further, "approximately 70% of contested custody cases [in the United States] that involve a history of domestic violence result in an award of sole or joint custody to the abuser" (Aiken & Murphy, 2000). This is an alarming statistic, which indicates that there are serious problems in the U.S. family court system. Many of these decisions are reversed on appeal, underscoring the importance of mandating training on domestic violence for trial court judges, and providing affordable appellate attorneys for victims of domestic violence. Note that we have no way of knowing how many cases—in which batterers were awarded custody or liberal visitation—were not appealed due to the victim's lack of funds.

A related area of law involves juvenile court cases in which the battered mother's parental rights are terminated due to her supposed "failure to protect" the child from witnessing her being abused; these cases are all too common, especially in the United States. Although this book does not focus on criminal juvenile court cases, such cases will be mentioned briefly.

Although the primary topic of this chapter is reported appellate decisions, discussion of some trial court decisions is also included. This is because many battered women going through custody and visitation battles have important contributions to make to our understanding of this problem, and their voices need to be heard. Additionally, because few trial court decisions are appealed, and only some appellate decisions are officially reported, it is useful to supplement these cases with trial court decisions that were not appealed, in order to have a more complete picture of the situation.

❖ UNITED STATES

"Best Interests of the Child"

Even under the minimal "best interest" analysis or a statute that merely "permits" the court to consider domestic violence, several recent U.S. cases hold that the abusive parent's violence was either the determining factor, or a significant factor, in awarding the other parent custody. However, in some instances, fathers receive custody, in spite of domestic violence allegations or proof that they have been abusive to their wives. For example, in *Telesco v. Telesco* (Ct. Superior Court 1996, unreported), 1996 WL 634288, the father was given custody because the trial court did not believe the mother's allegations of abuse; instead, the court found that the father was abused by the mother. An abusive father received custody in *Hilliard v. Peroni* (N.Y. App. Div., 1997), 666 N.Y.S.2d 92, because, even though both he and the mother enthusiastically participated in counselling, he also showed a willingness for the children to do so and the mother did not.

In some cases, the main factor appears to be which parent was the primary caretaker of the children before the parents separated. But even in such cases, domestic violence may be a factor in whether the court orders joint legal custody. In *Farrell v. Farrell* (Alaska 1991), 819 P.2d 896, the mother was the primary caretaker and was granted legal and physical custody. Because there was some evidence of mutual abuse between the parents, the court held that the history of domestic violence indicated that the parents were unable to share decision making, and joint custody was not appropriate.

Abuse by one of the parents toward a new partner is sometimes an important issue. For example, in *Lashbrook v. Lashbrook*, (Alaska, 1998), 957 P.2d 326, the mother sought to modify the joint legal and physical custody order, based on the father's assault of his new girlfriend. The mother was awarded temporary custody at a hearing in which the court found the assault had occurred in the children's presence. The father also pled no contest to the assault in the criminal court. However, the appellate court reversed the trial court's decision to make the temporary custody order permanent, holding that the father should have been provided with notice and a more in-depth hearing appropriate for a permanent custody modification.

As mentioned in Chapter 3, some batterers seek to use the family court system to continue to harass and control their ex-partners. For example, in *In re Marriage of Kim* (1989), 208 Cal. App. 3d 364, the trial court gave the father custody of the daughter, but reversed the order when he shot the mother—paralyzing her for life—and took the daughter to Korea. After the father returned to the United States, he was arrested for sexually and physically abusing the daughter and convicted of attempting to murder the wife, but never served much time in jail. Described by his parole officer as "a very polite, unobtrusive time bomb," this father sued everyone ever connected with the case, and even attempted to disqualify his ex-wife's attorney. In addition to disagreeing with every proposed visitation supervisor, the father appealed the denial of a jury trial in the custody case (in the United States such cases are always decided by judges alone), and alleged multiple violations of his civil rights. The court imposed sanctions on the father for his frivolous appeals, and published the decision to warn other courts about this man.

Although this case is rather extreme, it shows the lengths to which some batterers will go in litigating custody. Sometimes this type of activity is allowed to go on for years before courts interrupt it; in a few cases, the batterer is labelled a "vexatious litigant" and is no longer allowed to file lawsuits and motions without prior court approval.

Cases Decided Under Statutes Requiring That Domestic Violence Be Taken Into Account

In several cases, a statutory presumption against custody to a batterer, discussed in the previous chapter, was the determining factor in the custody decision. The North Dakota Supreme Court has decided many cases along these lines. In most of these cases, the batterer was denied custody. However, *Dinius v. Dinius* (N.D., 1997), 564 N.W.2d 300, held that the presumption was not raised by one minor violent incident occurring years before the separation. Cases from other states in which the presumption was key include *Russo v. Gardner* (Nev. 1998), 956 P.2d, and *McDermott v. McDermott* (Nev. 1997), 946 P.2d 177. In the case of *Jackson v. Jackson* (Ala. App., 1997), 709 So.2d 46, the court ruled that the statute creating a rebuttable presumption against custody to the batterer should be given more weight than the statute favoring joint custody.

Statutes may also forbid joint legal custody or shared decision making in domestic violence cases. Cases in which such legislation was key include *Marriage of C.M.C. and D.W.C.* (Wa. App. 1997), 940 P.2d 669, and *Caven v. Caven* (Wash. 1998), 966 P.2d 1247. Statutes may require written findings of fact about domestic violence. In *Custody of Vaughn* (Mass. 1996), 664 N.E.2d 434, custody to the batterer father was reversed due to failure to comply with this requirement.

A case showing how devious batterers can be in obtaining custody is *In Matter of JD v. ND* (N.Y. Fam. Ct. 1996), 652 N.Y.S.2d 468. In that case, the court gave custody to the battered mother, citing the new statute requiring the court to consider domestic violence. Other reasons for the decision included the father's alcoholism, his driving without a license, and his lying to the court about the whereabouts of the mother and child. He had told the court he had no idea where they were in his successful application for a temporary custody order, but then hired a private investigator to track the mother down to a domestic violence shelter. The investigator offered the mother money and a place to stay in another state; when the mother and child went there, the father arrived at the new location to pick up the child. The court exhibited a clear understanding of domestic violence dynamics, referring to the father's use of sexual abuse, psychological abuse, intimidation, isolation, and fear to control the victim.

In *In re M.R.* (Tex. App. 1998), 975 S.W.2d 51, domestic violence against the mother was the key issue in her obtaining custody, due to a statute requiring consideration of domestic violence if it occurred within the previous 2 years.

One of the issues discussed in the previous chapter was the tension between many states' "friendly parent" provisions, on the one hand, and taking domestic violence into account on the other. In some states, there are statutes mandating both policies at the same time, without guidance for judges as to how to handle the ensuing conflicts. *Ford v. Ford* (Fl. App. 1997), 700 So.2d 191, provides an example of a court decision in which this issue arose. In that case, the trial court had given custody to the batterer father, because the mother did not appear to be a "friendly parent," since she did not encourage extensive contact between the children and the father. The state statute specified that an important factor in the custody decision was which parent most encouraged contact with the other. The appellate court reversed the order, stating that the mother's lack of friendliness was due to her partner's abuse, and pointing out that the statute requires the court to consider domestic violence when determining shared parental responsibility. Thus, the statutory domestic violence provisions trumped the friendly parent provisions.

Visitation

There are many recent cases in the United States dealing with the issue of domestic violence in the context of visitation. As predicted in the previous chapter, courts are increasingly requiring that any visitation by serious batterers be supervised. In the last chapter, the Louisiana statute was described as the strictest regarding visitation in domestic violence cases. An example of how this statute is applied in court can be found in *Michelli v. Michelli* (La. App. 1995), 655 So.2d 1342, in which the trial court ordered unsupervised visitation to the father in spite of his history of domestic violence. The appellate court reversed this order and remanded the case to the trial court, directing the trial court to follow the statute, which requires supervised visitation until the batterer undergoes counseling.[4]

Courts are usually reluctant to terminate visitation altogether, even when domestic violence has occurred. For example, in *McCauley v. McCauley* (Ind. App. 1997), 678 N.E.2d 1290, the court held that the mother could not use the fact that the father had been violent to her before the divorce to modify the visitation order from supervised visitation to no visitation. And in *State v. Sturgeon* (Ohio Ct. App. 2000), 138 Ohio App. 3d 882, 2000 WL 1363182, the father was convicted of felony domestic violence against the mother. The sentence included an order to stay away from the child for 4 years, which was reversed on appeal because it effectively terminated the father's parental rights without the procedural guarantees required under state law.

Evidentiary Issues

Sometimes parties to custody or visitation disputes will ask a domestic violence expert to testify at the trial. This is done to educate the trier of fact (which, in family law cases, is the judge) about the effect of domestic violence on particular children, or on children generally. Use of such testimony was upheld in *Knock v. Knock* (Ct. 1993), 621 A.2d 267, and was mentioned with approval in *Brainard v. Brainard* (Ia. App. 1994), 523 N.W.2d 611.

However, an appellate judge voiced concern about the general use of experts in custody cases in *Keesee v. Keesee* (Fla. Dist. Ct. App. 1996), 675 So.2d 655, in which the battered mother was awarded custody. Use of experts is not necessarily required in such cases. For example, in *Berg v. Berg* (N.D. 2000), 606 N.W.2d 895, the North Dakota Supreme Court held that the battered custodial mother was not required to present expert testimony to show that unsupervised visitation with the more violent parent would harm the child. Courts can always take judicial notice of any legislative findings made by legislatures, which can be another way to get expert opinion information before courts.

Parental Alienation Syndrome

As discussed in Chapter 2, the new phenomenon of Parental Alienation Syndrome (PAS), developed by physician Richard Gardner, has come under a great deal of scrutiny. Although many professionals in the field maintain that it does not exist, it is often used in cases in which the alienated parent has caused the alienation through abuse of the child, the other parent, or both. A similar analysis to PAS, but one even more obviously misogynist, is the so-called "Malicious Mother Syndrome," a recent development. The gender bias in both analyses is overwhelming: One researcher noted that she was unable to find a single reported case where PAS testimony was introduced on behalf of the mother (Wood, 1994).

Cases in which PAS is raised frequently involve domestic violence. For example, in one trial court case in which Dr. Gardner testified that a mother had alienated her children from their father, the facts showed that the father had shot the mother 13 times during the custody battle. A commentator noted that this "is a fairly good indication that something else may have caused or contributed to his children's alienation from him" (Wood, 1994, p. 1415). Ironically, even Dr. Gardner admits in his books that PAS is inappropriate in any cases involving domestic violence.

Courts in the United States are starting to address the issue of PAS. Although many courts have upheld trial court rulings based in part on PAS evidence, appellate courts in at least three states have held that this "syndrome" is too controversial to be accepted. In the first reported case to reject PAS evidence, *In the Interest of TMW* (Florida 1989), 533 So.2d 260, 262, the court stated: "No determination was made in the order or on the record as to general professional acceptance of the 'parental alienation syndrome' as a diagnostic tool. . . . [W]e note the cautionary words of other current commentators. . . [E]xperts have not achieved consensus on the existence of a psychological syndrome that can detect child sexual abuse." The court also cited the causation and proof problems inherent in this type of analysis, noting that these problems are the reason the old cause of action for "alienation of affection" between spouses is no longer allowed in most U.S. states.

In another case, *Wiederholt v. Fischer* (Wis. 1992), 485 N.W.2d 442, the appellate court left the children with the mother despite the testimony of the father's psychologist that this was one of the worst cases of PAS by a mother that he had ever seen. Among its reasons for affirming the trial court's refusal to transfer custody to the father, the appellate court noted the "limited research data," which supported the removal of the children from their mother's custody, "as a successful cure" for severe PAS. However, it is still troubling that the court admitted the PAS testimony at all, given the serious issues as to whether PAS even exists. Some experts in the field have called it "junk science" and maintain that it does not comply with the U.S. Supreme Court's rules about expert scientific testimony. This concern is in addition to the gender bias demonstrated in all the reported PAS cases (Wood, 1994).

In another case where PAS testimony was disallowed, *People v. Loomis* (N.T. App. 1997), 658 N.Y.S.2d 787, the parties were undergoing a divorce, and the father was criminally charged with sexually abusing the children. He asked the criminal trial court for an order requiring the wife and children to submit to psychiatric examinations from Dr. Richard Gardner, who planned to testify about PAS at the trial. The court refused this request, stating that New York had not ever admitted such testimony. Further, no state statute allowed a criminal defendant to force the alleged victims to undergo psychiatric examination, and the reason for the request did not conform to New York evidence laws. This was because Dr. Gardner purported to be able to determine the truth of the accusation from his examination, and planned to testify accordingly. The laws of evidence in all U.S. states leave this determination to the trier of fact, so expert testimony must be limited to generalities and the effects of any admissible syndrome.

Relocation and Parental Childsnatching Within the United States

As discussed in the previous chapter, a major issue in some domestic violence cases is a request by the victim of domestic violence to relocate to a new community with the children. Or the victim may move without such court permission. Such a move may be key in building a new, safe life, closer to the mother's support system. It may also allow her to remarry or pursue higher education or employment.[5]

Historically, husbands in the United States had the right to decide where the family would live; this right seems to have carried over into modern postdivorce decisions. Although the current rationale for this right is "the best interest of the child," to ensure frequent and continuing contact with both parents, the real motive in many cases appears to be protecting the father's right to control where the ex-wife and children live. And, as previously noted, frequent and continuing contact with both parents is often not advisable in domestic violence situations.

In one case described by Janet Bowermaster, even though the husband was convicted of domestic violence against the wife, it took 2½ years of ongoing court battles before the judge gave the wife permission to relocate with the child from California to Florida. During this time, three custody evaluators and the child's therapist recommended that the move be allowed, and the husband continued to harass and stalk the wife on many occasions—causing the wife to lose her job and rely on public assistance. The wife was told by a prosecutor that if she took her child and left without the court's permission she could be charged with federal kidnapping and lose her child. She ended up owing a great deal of money and filing for bankruptcy, and the child suffered serious psychological harm, before they were finally allowed to move (Bowermaster, 1998).

In many cases, mothers do not wait for court permission, but, rather, just take the children and flee. Although trial courts may look harshly on this type of action, appellate courts may not. For example, in *Marriage of Marconi* (Iowa 1998), 584 N.W.2d 331, the mother and child fled the state to avoid abuse. In the mother's absence, and without notice to her, the husband obtained a dissolution and custody decree. In vacating this order, the state Supreme Court cited three similar cases, and ruled that fear for the mother's and child's safety justified the mother's leaving. See, also, *Vachon v. Pugliese* (Alaska 1996), 931 P.2d 371, in which the Alaska trial court awarded the stalking father custody—after the mother secretly fled with the child to Massachusetts—stating that she had committed custodial interference. The appellate court reversed this decision, finding that the mother had not acted wrongfully.

Mothers who flee with children are not always treated with understanding by the appellate courts. For example, in *Larson v. Dunn* (Minn. 1990), 460 N.W.2d 39, the mother lost temporary physical custody after fleeing with the daughter and hiding for 7 years. When they were found and forced to return, the mother said that she fled due to domestic violence, as well as the father's physical and sexual abuse of the daughter. The court held that the mother did not have sufficient cause to flee. Custody was given to the father, and the mother did not see the daughter for several years. The father even went so far as to sue the mother and her parents for intentional infliction of emotional distress, fraud, conspiracy, and intentional interference with custodial rights.

Although the court refused to allow the father to sue for this last cause of action, it is unclear whether he prevailed on the other claims.

Mothers who are victims of domestic violence generally take their children with them when fleeing from their abusers. Besides leading to a custody dispute, this can result in criminal charges of childsnatching. For example, in *Bruscato v. Avant* (La. App. 1995), 660 So.2d 471, the father succeeded in having the mother arrested for fleeing the state with the child, and also obtained custody due to the "lack of stability" she demonstrated by fleeing. However, the appellate court remanded the case back to the trial court because the legislature had just passed a new law creating a presumption against granting custody to a batterer.

Additionally, fathers who are batterers sometimes abduct children. See, for example, *Strother v. Alaska* (Alaska App. 1995), 891 P.2d 214, in which the father was convicted of custodial interference after he took the child, threatening that the mother would never see the child again. It is notable that this occurred soon after a protective order was issued against the father, the time period in which domestic violence cases often escalate in severity.

Fleeing Across International Lines: Cases Decided Under the Hague Convention

When victims of domestic violence flee with their children from their abusers, they may remain in the same state or province, cross state lines, or even cross international lines. The international cases often arise when a U.S. citizen marries a foreign national, moves with the spouse to the foreign country, and then is abused in the foreign country. The U.S. citizen is most likely to want to return to her home country, close to her family and support system—the same reason most battered women flee with children across state lines.

If victims of domestic violence cross state lines but stay in the United States, the case triggers the Uniform Child Custody Jurisdiction and Enforcement Act or the older Uniform Child Custody Jurisdiction Act. If they cross international lines, the Hague Convention on the Civil Aspects of International Child Abduction comes into play. Each country signing the convention, including the United States, Canada, New Zealand, and Australia, agrees to abide by its provisions.

As mentioned in Chapter 3, although the main emphasis of the Convention is to ensure that any wrongfully removed child under age 16 is returned to his or her "habitual residence," there are exceptions if "there is a grave risk that his or her return would expose the child to physical or psychological harm or otherwise place the child in an intolerable situation." Several of the earlier U.S. cases held that any grave risk must involve war, famine, or disease, and rejected domestic violence as a basis for allowing the child to stay in the new country. Indeed, the "grave risk exception has been narrowly interpreted by the vast majority of courts to apply only when returning children to parts of the world that are unsafe because of war or natural disaster, rather than to abusive parents" (see Perry & Zorza, 2001). In some domestic violence situations, however, U.S. courts have applied the grave risk exception, with mixed results.

For example, domestic violence toward the mother was found to be grounds for grave risk to the children in *Blondin v. Dubois* (S.D.N.Y. 2000), 78 F. Supp. 2d 283, and *Walsh v. Walsh* (1st Cir. 2000), 221 F.3d 204. In other cases, courts take the domestic violence seriously but attempt to arrange a safe way for the custody decision to be made in the home country. For example, in *Turner v. Frowein* (Ct. 2000), 752 A.2d 955, the case was remanded to the U.S. trial court to evaluate placement options and legal safeguards in the home country before the order determining which country would make the custody decision was issued.

In *Tabacchi v. Harrison* (N.D. Ill. 2000), 2000 WL 190576, the federal district court found that there was no grave risk to the child, in spite of the father's abuse of the mother, and ordered the child's return to Italy. The father had promised to provide separate housing, a car, and child support in Italy. This approach is referred to by the courts as an "undertaking," and appears to be part of a new trend in this area of law. (One wonders, of course, if such promises can be relied on or enforced.) The U.S. court found no reason to believe the father would disobey any Italian protective orders or that the Italian authorities would fail to protect the mother and child.

In a third category of cases, courts simply find there is no grave risk to the child and order the child to be returned to the home country without any "undertaking." Examples include *Croll v. Croll* (S.D. N.Y. 1999), 66 F. Supp. 2d 554, *Janakakis-Kostun v. Janakakis* (Ky. Ct. App. 1999), 6 S.W.3d 843, and *Dalmasso v. Dalmasso* (Kan. 2000), 9 P.3d 551.

The lower levels of abuse in these cases may have been significant in this outcome.

Third Parties: New Partners, Grandparents

In some cases, nonbiological parents or nonparents are parties to the custody or visitation dispute. Domestic violence may be a key factor in these cases as well.[6]

The most famous U.S. case to deal with grandparents seeking guardianship over the wishes of a batterer is *Guardianship of Simpson* (Cal. App. 1998) 67 Cal. App. 4th 914. In that case, the grandparents had been awarded temporary guardianship of the grandchildren while the father, O. J. Simpson, was on trial for the murder of the mother, Nicole Brown Simpson. After his acquittal, but pending a civil suit for wrongful death, the trial court terminated the guardianship, returning the children to the father. The grandparents appealed, and the appellate court reversed the termination, holding that it was reversible error to exclude evidence of the mother's murder and her diaries. It also directed the trial court to determine whether the father had "a propensity for domestic violence," which it found extremely important in determining the father's fitness. The court stated that the trial court had used the wrong standard for termination of a guardianship, because the burden of proof should have been on the party seeking to terminate the guardianship, not on the guardians.

Note also that the U.S. Supreme Court greatly limited state laws regarding grandparent visitation in *Troxel v. Granville*, 530 U.S. 57 (2000). While this case did not involve domestic violence, it raised the issue of whether grandparents had the right to visit with their grandchildren over the objection of the custodial parent. This scenario sometimes arises in cases where the batterer's parents seek to continue contact with the child(ren) over the objection of the battered mother. In such situations, the grandparents may be requesting visitation so their son, the batterer, can continue to have contact with the child(ren) even when the court has cut off the father's visitation rights.

Due to the high rates of divorce and remarriage in the United States, stepparent issues frequently arise in custody and visitation cases involving domestic violence. Courts appear to be prone to deprive mothers of custody if they marry batterers, or to deprive fathers of custody if they batter a new wife. For example, the mother's right to marry a known child abuser/batterer was the issue in *Mishlen v. Mishlen* (N.J. Super. 1997), 702 A.2d 1384, in which the mother was ordered to choose between her abusive fiancé and her children. See also *In the Interest of L.B.* (Iowa App. 1995), 530 N.W.2d 465, in which the biological father was given permanent custody of the child after the mother failed to comply with reunification services. The mother's rights were terminated due to her refusal to accept help to improve the dangerous conditions at home with her new abusive husband. However, in *Holmes v. Greene* (Fla. App. 1995), 649 So.2d 302, the mother was allowed to continue as custodian after divorcing her abusive second husband before the hearing. In *Halverson v. Taflin* (Minn. Ct. App. 2000) 617 N.W.2d 448, the father filed for an ex parte restraining order against the mother's boyfriend, alleging that the boyfriend had been violent toward the mother and requesting a change of custody from the mother to the father based on this abuse. The court granted the temporary change in custody. The appellate court reversed this order, holding that the mother should have been allowed to intervene as a party in the suit.

In all these cases, courts are giving great weight to the history of domestic violence between the adults. It is clear that they are concerned about the effects on children of living with such abuse, regardless of whether the children are directly abused.

Termination of Parental Rights by Juvenile Courts

In many recent U.S. cases, men who were abusive to their children's mothers have had their parental rights terminated by juvenile courts.[7] However, a surprising line of cases shows courts bending over backward to give batterer fathers more chances to parent, in some cases even giving them custody.[8] It is very rare for fathers to face criminal charges for failing to protect children from abusive mothers, which suggests gender bias in the legal system. When it comes to protecting children, mothers are held to a much higher standard than fathers. (See, however, *People v. Malone* (N.Y. Crim. Ct. 1999), 683 N.T.S.2d 390, in which the batterer father was charged with child endangerment for assaulting the mother in front of the child.)

Similarly, one attorney reported what is clearly a reality throughout the United States: "In 16 years of working in the courts, she had never seen a father even charged with 'failure to protect' when the child abuser was the mother. In a classic example of legally sanctioned gender bias, it is mothers, not fathers, who find themselves facing such charges. Fathers who abandon their children rarely face criminal responsibility" (Davidson, 1995). An example of this is found in *In re L.G. et al.* (Okla. App. 1993), 854 P.2d 1301, in which the father had abused the mother in front of the child and the mother had abused the child. The child was removed from the home, the mother's parental rights were terminated, and the father was given a service plan to complete in order to qualify to be the custodial parent. He did not complete the plan, and his parental rights were terminated. The appellate court reversed the termination of the father's parental rights, stating that even though he may have failed to protect the child from the mother, this issue was not raised at trial, so it had not been found to be a cause of the child's being deprived. Thus, even when it appeared that the father had been abusive to the mother and had failed to protect the child from the abusive mother, the father was not charged with a crime and his parental rights were not terminated.

Although family courts are increasingly awarding custody to battered mothers (at least at the appellate level), in juvenile courts, battered mothers appear to be much more likely to lose their children through termination of their parental rights. Courts frequently find that these women are unable to protect their children from witnessing abuse or being directly abused by the mother's partner (who may not be the father). Instead of giving up on battered mothers whose fitness is being questioned, programs are needed to assist them to protect their children.

The most extreme example of inappropriately blaming a mother for her own abuse is found in *In the Matter of Aimee Janine Farley* (Mich. 1991), 469 N.W.2d 295, in which the children and mother were abused by the father. The mother obtained a divorce from the batterer, went to counseling, and got a court order stating that the only contact between the father and children would be with a supervisor present. In spite of all these protections, the juvenile court terminated the mother's parental rights, based merely on a concern that she might marry another batterer. This decision was based on the myth "once a battered woman, always a battered woman," which was voiced by psychologists and social workers in the case. Although one justice of the state supreme court wrote a long opinion arguing for reversal, the other justices declined to review this outrageous decision. The case has been soundly criticized by many commentators, but has never been overturned.

In many cases, both parents' parental rights may be terminated due to child abuse by the father and neglect by the battered mother.[9] Even more troubling are the cases in which the children are not directly abused by the mother's partner, but the mother's parental rights are terminated due to "secondary abuse." This term signifies that the children have witnessed the abuse of their parent, usually the mother. These cases blame the battered mother for the actions of her batterer, and emphasize the need for caution when we employ phrases such as "witnessing domestic violence is child abuse." Although useful, this concept must be presented within a larger context.

In *In re the Matter of Theresa CC* (N.Y. Supreme Ct. App. Div. 1991), 576 N.Y.S.2d 937, both parents were found guilty of emotional neglect for exposing their children to domestic violence on many occasions. (Note that although the court characterized the violence as mutual, studies show this is rare, with most physical violence by women actually being self-defense.) More typical is *In re Lonell J* (N.Y. App. Div. 1998), 673 N.Y.S.2d 116, in which the battered mother was found to have emotionally neglected her children because they witnessed her being abused by the father, in spite of evidence that police were called repeatedly, the father was arrested, and a protective order was issued. And in the *Matter of Deandre T.* (N.Y. App. Div. 1998), 253 A.D.2d 497, the father's abuse of the mother in front of one of their children was sufficient to sustain a finding of neglect of that child's sibling. Obviously, such outcomes have a chilling effect on battered mothers ever seeking help for the abuse.

On the other hand, sometimes the mother's parental rights are reinstated by the appellate court. In *In the Matter of Nina A.M.* (N.Y. Supreme Ct. App. Div. 1993), 593 N.Y.S.2d 89, the mother was found by the trial court to have neglected the children because, the state argued, she should have been aware of the abuse and taken action to prevent it. This was reversed on appeal, because the mother had acted prudently and reasonably in leaving the abusive father and moving to another city to be further away from him—before the petition alleging child abuse was filed. It is notable that, in this case, the court saw the mother's relocation as a positive action.

In a recent class action decision, *In re Shawrline, Nicholson, et al.* (2002), 181 F. Supp. 2d 182, a federal district court enjoined the New

York City Administration for Children's Services (ACS) from removing children from their battered mothers based solely on the children having witnessed the abuse. ACS had characterized these battered mothers as having "engaged in domestic violence." The court held that the practice of removing the children on this basis violated the constitutional right of parents and children not to be separated by the government unless the parent is found to be unfit. Although this case technically applies only to New York City, it clearly has national significance, as the constitutional right raised in it belongs to all parents and children in the United States.

Courts also often place custody with the murderer's parents or family without assessing them for domestic violence or how supportive they were of the father's abuse of the child's mother (APA, p. 80, *Violence in the Family*).

In many cases in which the mother is charged with failing to protect the child from her partner, the outcome depends on whether the mother knew about the child abuse. In some cases, the question becomes not whether she knew of it, but whether she "should have known" of it, a questionable basis on which to convict someone of a crime.[10] These cases show attempts by battered women to introduce evidence concerning their inability to prevent the child abuse. In some instances, as in *People v. Lemons* (Mich. 1997), 562 N.W.2d 447, the defense is duress, with the defendant claiming she was threatened with great bodily injury or death if she intervened. In other cases (e.g., *Commonwealth v. Lazarovich* (Mass. 1991), 574 N.E.2d 340), expert witnesses in the arena of domestic violence are brought in to explain why the mother was unable to stop the child abuse. It is rare, however, that such defenses result in acquittals. (See, e.g., *In re the Matter of Glenn G.* (N.Y. Fam. Ct. 1992), 587 N.Y.S.2d 464.)

In the most extreme domestic violence cases, the batterer kills the mother of his children. Surprisingly, even when these men are convicted, many of them contest the termination of their parental rights. The pre-1990 court decisions in this area seem to be based on how long the batterer will be incarcerated. A troubling number of courts have held that killing the coparent is not sufficient to terminate parental rights.[11] In *Wolfe v. Wolfe* (Nev. 1999), 972 P.2d 1138, contact with the child was allowed over the objection of the mother, who had survived attempted murder by the father. Recent cases, however, indicate that courts appear to be more willing to terminate parental rights in cases where the father has killed the mother.[12]

This issue rarely arises in the context of a mother killing her coparent. This may be attributable to the lower incidence of women killing men than of men killing women. It may also be that women's parental rights are not generally terminated under these conditions, or that women whose parental rights are terminated in these circumstances either do not appeal the termination or arrange to place their children with appropriate guardians while they are incarcerated.

❖ NEW ZEALAND

Overview: Historical Custody Cases

In general, custody cases between parents in New Zealand from the 1970s, 1980s, and early 1990s show that courts treated domestic violence as a nonissue. When they did consider domestic violence to be relevant to custody or access (visitation), the focus was on the physical violence only; other aspects of abuse, such as controlling behavior, were invisible. Two prominent researchers from New Zealand state,

> There was a view among many judges that one could be a violent spouse (even a spouse killer) but still be a good parent. Custody and access decisions were frequently made as if a parent's violence was irrelevant to his ability to provide a physically and psychologically safe environment for children; this despite repeated research findings concerning the statistical relationship between spouse and child abuse and the deleterious effect on children of witnessing domestic violence. In many cases, the children were further abused, either directly by the abuser or indirectly as the children witnessed assaults on their mothers at access change-over times. (Busch & Robertson, 2000)

Unfortunately, the judges themselves seem to have adopted the rationalizations of the batterers regarding the violence. In many cases, they saw the violence as being based in the relationship, rather than a problem caused by the batterer. The judges sometimes minimized the violence or erased it completely in their decisions.

For example, in *N v. N* (1986) 2 FRNZ 534, the former husband applied to the court for an order stating that the child should be enrolled in Catholic school, even though the custodial mother was not Catholic. The husband was in prison for having raped the wife after they had separated—something he had done on several occasions. There had also been a nonmolestation order in effect. In spite of this domestic violence history, the court ordered what the father requested, characterizing the violence as "the parties' discord," and "the parties [becoming] so out of tune with each other that events were allowed to develop as they did." This is a classic example of minimization of abuse. The court also stressed the need for the mother to "consider the father's position as coguardian." Throughout the case, the court emphasized the father's rights, equating them with the best interest of the child, and ignored the impact of the decision on the mother in her role as custodial parent.

In a 1991 unreported criminal case, *R. v. Panoa-Masina* (CA Ct. of Appeals, 7 October 1991; CA 309/91; see, also, Busch & Robertson, 2000), both the trial and appellate courts assumed that even a father who is homicidally violent to his partner can be a fit custodial parent. The father was convicted of manslaughter after beating his partner of 12 years so severely that she died a few days later. The trial court sentence was only 9 months periodic (noncustodial) detention; the appellate court doubled this to 18 months, which is still extremely light compared with other manslaughter sentences in New Zealand. One reason the court gave for the sentence was that the parties had an 8-year-old son. If the father was imprisoned, the son would "temporarily lose the advantage of the guidance and companionship of his only surviving parent." Nowhere in the decision is there any reference to whether a man who has beaten the mother of his child to death would be a good parent. Nor is there any mention of where the boy was during the beating. The boy had 13 half-siblings, all adults, who could have cared for him.

In response to national public outcry over the lack of awareness on the part of the judiciary, the Domestic Violence Act and major amendments to the Guardianship Act were adopted in 1995, as described in Chapter 3. These statutory changes have contributed to a "shift . . . away from a concentration on physical violence in heterosexual marriage-like relationships to an emphasis on prohibiting the use of a myriad of tactics of power and control against a diverse range of domestic violence victims" (Busch & Robertson, 2000).

Three recent trial court cases illustrate this shift in awareness. In the first case, *D v. D* (1997) NZFLR 673, the mother had custody of her 2-year-old twins and the father was seeking supervised access. Taking the history of violence toward both the mother and children seriously, the court refused even this limited form of access, stating that a precondition was the father's responsibility to effectively stop his violent behavior. The judge noted the father's minimization of his violent behavior in his court pleadings, and his blaming the mother for having "provoked" him. The judge also focused on the mother's perception of the nature and seriousness of the violence, and its effects on her and the children, as mandated by the new statutes. This included giving great weight to the father's threats, many of which had been carried out in the past. The judge also did not agree that mere participation in a batterers' treatment program was indicative of the father's actually starting to deal with his power and control issues. In fact, the father had threatened to kill the mother after he was enrolled in such a program. The court also stated that the father had used supervised access for the purposes of attempting to persuade the mother to reconcile. Interestingly, the court also found that the posttraumatic stress disorder that the mother suffered from, far from impeding her caregiving role, was a factor indicating that the father's access to the children should be denied. The court held that, due to all these reasons, there was too much emotional strain on the 2-year-old twins and their mother to permit even supervised access at that point in time.

In *Cocker v. Middleton* (1997) NZFLR 113, the mother sought custody after the parents had initially agreed that the abusive father should have custody. During and after the separation, the father had been violent to the mother, often in front of the children. He had also threatened and intimidated her, which the court found significant. In spite of having been convicted of two of these incidents, the father continued to portray himself as blameless, characterizing the mother as having deserved the abuse. Similar to the *D v. D* case, the father had enrolled in a short-term batterers' program, but it did not seem to be affecting his attitude. Showing a sophisticated understanding of the dynamics of domestic violence, the court expressed concern about the father's feeling that he had the "right to retain control of the situation."

This understanding may have been facilitated by the inclusion of psychological abuse in the Domestic Violence Act statutory definition of domestic violence. It appears that the court granted the mother custody, with supervised access to the father.

The third case, *Gill v. Welsh* (Family Court at Wellington, unreported, 1996; see, also, Busch & Robertson, 2000), also involved an abusive father seeking access to the child, who was in the custody of his mother. The father had a long history of physical abuse toward the mother and child, including several convictions, as well as having abused other partners. The mother cut off access after the father assaulted her friend in front of the child; the court interpreted the assault as psychological abuse of the mother and child through intimidation. The father was also sexually abusing the child. The court assessed the risk of the father having unsupervised access to the child, using the newly enacted statutory language and its prioritization of child safety over any other matters. Although there had been no physical abuse of the mother in the previous 2½ years, the judge acknowledged the ongoing threats and intimidation as very significant. The judge also looked at the contexts in which the father had become violent, his minimization of his violence, his blaming his violence on others, his apparent unconcern for the effect of his behavior on his child, and his focus on the "rights of a father." The judge also found unpersuasive the father's attendance at 12 weeks of "anger-management" classes. The court concluded that, although these classes may have helped him stop the physical violence, "it is plain to see that Mr. Welsh has not learned the techniques or has not chosen to use them in relation to controlling intimidation and the inappropriate expression of his anger." For all these reasons, the court ordered only supervised access through a center that provided this service.

Although these three cases are exemplary, Busch and Robertson state,

> Our research also has shown that some old problems remain and, as batterers respond to the new statutory provisions, new problems are appearing. We have seen recently decided cases which continue to suggest that victims "provoke" domestic violence incidents. We have seen judgments where the causes of violence within a relationship continue to be attributed to communication problems between the parties. We have also seen judgments where

> women have been characterized as suffering from battered women's syndrome and this has been used to justify the removal of children from their custody. (Busch & Robertson, 2000)

An example of this is *Bayly v. Bayly* (Family Court at Christchurch, unreported, 1997; FP 0009/1537/92, 23 May 1997; see, also, Busch & Robertson, 2000). The wife had been refused two prior nonmolestation orders, which the court characterized as unnecessary, and was also denied her third request. This occurred in spite of the husband's admissions of physical violence and repetitive stalking. The husband also kept the child at an unknown address during access, and the court-appointed psychologist found that the child did not want to see her father, was afraid of him, and appeared to be suffering from posttraumatic stress disorder. Nevertheless, the court saw the wife as being anti-male, and as having provoked the husband's physical abuse of herself and her mother—in the presence of the child—by denying him access. The court said the husband was a "meek and mild person who would not willingly assault anyone," and praised him for having assaulted his wife only once in 5 years. The court continued unsupervised access, and recommended 3 or 4 months of counselling for both parents, separately.

A similar case was *Simmons v. Foote* (Family Court at Wanganui, unreported, (1997); FP 083/280/95, 8 April 1997; see, also, Busch & Robertson, 2000), which also arose in the context of a protection order application. In that case, the judge excused the father's postseparation harassment and stalking of the mother, some of which was witnessed by the children, stating that each parent was responsible for the abuse and that this was a "communication" problem. Although he granted the mother's request for a protection order, the judge also clarified that "the making of the protection order does not in any way enhance the applicant's right to retain custody of the children. . . .The protection order relates to problems that exist between the applicant and the respondent and on that point I note it was adopted by the applicant that there was no issue of any physical abuse arising in this context." This judge seems to be unaware of the recent statutory changes in New Zealand defining domestic violence as including psychological abuse.

The third case, *L v. S* (1997) FLRNZ 550, involved a battered mother seeking custody of her daughter, who had been in the care of the father for 2½ years. In spite of the father's history of physical abuse of the mother, including a conviction for assault, the judge continued the custody with the father. The court stated that the mother "was not entirely blameless" for the assault, and characterized her as having acquiesced in whatever wrongs the husband had committed when she followed him to New Zealand and tried to reconcile with him. The judge stated that there was little likelihood of further abuse if the parties "remain separated and apart." Additionally, there was no evidence that the father was violent to the children. A psychologist determined that the children exhibited Parental Alienation Syndrome from their mother, and characterized this as a form of psychological abuse by the father, saying he showed a "pathological dependence upon his children." As noted earlier, it is very rare for PAS to be attributed to a father. The judge disagreed with the expert's recommendation that the daughter live with her mother, and twisted the cultural aspects of the case. The judge gave great weight to the testimony of the children's counselor, who said that Taiwanese culture places great value on not losing face or airing family matters in public. The judge consequently found that the mother had violated important Taiwanese cultural norms, in effect blaming her for asking the court for help to protect herself and her children. He also said she had not "promoted the whole family" and was not "supportive of the father."

The last case, *E v. S* (1997) FLRNZ 550 (described by Busch & Robertson, 2000), also involved severe violence by the father against the mother, her parents, and the children—with ongoing threats to abduct the children. The mother had obtained six nonmolestation orders, but then reconciled with the father. There were 60 police reports about the father, including a charge of threatening to kill a police officer. The parties again separated; when the mother agreed to the father having unsupervised access, the children were taken away from her by the family court. During court proceedings, the judge asked for police presence and the police themselves sent three officers. Even in this environment, the father was "antagonistic and threatening" in court. Because he represented himself, he was allowed to cross-examine all the witnesses, including the mother. Instead of finding that the legal system had failed to help this mother and children, the judge found that she was suffering from battered women's syndrome, impairing her ability to protect the children. The court did not make a final determination regarding whether the children could live with the mother, but expressed concern that if the children and the mother lived with her parents, all of them might be unsafe from the father. Busch and Robertson aptly characterize this as a case in which the victim of domestic violence and her children "pay the price for the lack of adequate protection afforded them" by the legal system (Busch & Robertson, 2000).

The Hague Convention Cases

As a signatory to the Hague Convention on Child Abduction, New Zealand courts also deal with international custody cases involving domestic violence. However, in the only two reported cases as of early 2001, the New Zealand courts have found no grave risk and ordered that the children be returned to their home countries.

In the first case, *Damiano v. Damiano* (1993) NZFLR 548, 1993 NZFLR Lexis 92, the mother was from New Zealand and the father was Canadian. They married in Canada and had three daughters. After the father threatened to kill the daughters, and on another occasion assaulted and threatened to kill the mother, the mother fled with the children to New Zealand. At the time, the children were ages 11, 8, and 6. During the trial, the court showed little understanding of the dynamics of domestic violence, describing the abuse as "unhappiness" and "strain," and regretting that "no counseling was sought." Acknowledging that the children seemed to be genuinely afraid of their father, the court also referred to "the steady escalation of power imbalance and threat" by the father, his "tyranny of temperament," and his "rather classic expression of the male privilege to control the lives of the woman and children of his household." The court also acknowledged the need to reorganize the family so the mother and children could feel safe.

The court made the return order conditional on several undertakings by the husband, including his vacating the family home and having only supervised access with the children until the Canadian courts could make a determination. The court issued a protective order against the father, and stated that he was in need of anger-management classes or counselling for his tendency toward violence. It also held the father to his promise not to initiate any criminal proceedings against his wife for taking the children. The court stated that the fact that all three children expressed a fear of their father and desired to stay in New Zealand was not dispositive, especially considering how young two of the children were. The court further noted that the Ontario legislation in place at the time, the Children's Law Reform Act, clearly provided for the custody and access determination to be made based on the best interests of the child, with consideration given to factors that would be also be considered by New Zealand courts.

The second case, *S v. S*, 3 NZLR 513 (1999), involved a mother who fled to New Zealand from Australia with her three children. The court also found that, in this case, there was no "grave risk" if the children were returned. The parties married in Fiji and lived there for 6 years, then lived in Australia for 10 years. At the time of separation, they had three children, ages 11, 13, and 15. After enduring years of physical and psychological abuse from the husband, which the children witnessed, the wife fled with the children to her family in New Zealand. When the husband petitioned the New Zealand court to order the wife and children to return to Australia, the Family Court found that there was a grave risk to the children. This was based on the husband's long-term abuse of the wife, the children's exposure to the violence, and the likelihood that the husband would become violent to the children if they crossed him. The court also found that such return would place the children in an intolerable situation. It further found that without the support of her brothers, the wife would be unable to stand up to the husband in an Australian custody court, due to her mental fragility (caused by the abuse), whereas the husband could effectively participate in proceedings in New Zealand.

However, the first court of appeal in New Zealand (the High Court of Auckland) reversed this decision, stating among other reasons, that it wanted to "demonstrat[e] to potential abductors that there is no future in interstate abductions." The court gave great weight to the maturity of the three children and their wish to return to their friends, home, and schools, stating that this was the decisive factor in its decision. It also stressed that the issue in such cases is not whether allowing custody or access to one parent would involve a grave risk to the child, but whether the legal system in the home country can be entrusted to safeguard the child's interests. Thus, even if the husband had been very abusive to the wife and was likely to be physically abusive to the children, this was not sufficient grounds to hold the custody proceedings in New Zealand. The Court of Appeal in Wellington, New Zealand, affirmed the intermediate court decision.

❖ CANADA

Overview

Similar to courts in the United States and New Zealand, cases in Canada—until the late 1980s—tended not to address domestic violence as a custody or access factor, and also tended to discount any allegations along these lines (Bala, 2001). However, this is starting to change, with courts increasingly taking domestic violence seriously, believing the battered party, and considering domestic violence to be relevant in custody and access cases. As discussed in the previous chapter, Canada has not adopted legislation explicitly addressing domestic violence as a custody or access factor, with the exception of a provincial statute in Newfoundland. However, many judges appear to be applying more modern concepts to these decisions even in the absence of statutory mandates. No doubt this change is due in part to training from Canadian domestic violence experts and advocates, which has taken place over the last 10 years.

Custody and Access

One of the first reported cases dealing with the effects of domestic violence on children was *Young v. Young* (1989) 19 RFL (3d) 227 (Ont. S.C.). There was a history of significant emotional abuse, sexual abuse, and two physical assaults by the father toward the mother after the parents separated. This abuse was taken seriously by the trial court in awarding the mother custody of the children. The court stated that "[a]n abuser who goes without therapy will continue to abuse in another relationship; [c]hildren who witness abuse can become abused even though the abuse is not intentionally directed at them; [and] [a]bused male children often become abusers and abused female children may become compliant to abusers." The father was awarded liberal but structured access. This case represents a number of Canadian cases in which custody was awarded to the abused mother.[13]

On the one hand, joint custody is often ordered in domestic violence cases, sometimes due to a "friendly parent" analysis. Courts in these cases seem unaware of how much cooperation is required to create and sustain a joint custody arrangement.[14] In some cases, however, joint custody was found to be inappropriate because of a history of significant disagreement, argument, and/or abuse.[15] This was the outcome in the one case found in which the mother had been violent toward the father.[16]

In some cases, abusive fathers are awarded custody. In *Worden v. Worden* (1994), 154 NBR (2d) 60 (Q.B. Fam. Div.) this occurred despite the father's abusiveness and alcoholism, on the condition that he receive counseling for his drinking and tendency toward violence. It appears that the daughter's preference to live with her father may well have been based on his possession of the family home; the mother was in a shelter with the son, who preferred to stay with her. The case is an example of the need for more low-cost or free legal services for victims of domestic violence; "the decision might well have been different if the mother had initially secured exclusive possession of the family home" (Bala, 2001).

Of course, access is also a major issue in these cases. In some recent Canadian cases, the court denied all access by the batterer, due in part to his lethality,[17] or to the children's expressed fear of their father.[18] In other cases, the court attempted supervised or unsupervised access but later cut it off.[19] In another group of cases, even completion of a batterers' program did not improve the father's behavior enough to continue access.[20]

On the other hand, there are also many cases in which courts granted access in spite of a history of domestic violence. In some such cases, any access is ordered to be supervised.[21] In certain circumstances, unsupervised access may be seen as appropriate. In *Brusselers v. Shiri* (1996), AJ 333 (Q.B.), the father's having already started counseling for his violence and the child's wish to see her father seem to have been key factors in the court's decision to grant the father unsupervised access to the child.

When batterers are awarded custody, they may use the award to continue their abuse, intimidation, and control of the partner, thwarting the other parent's attempts to see the children and emotionally abusing the children. For example, in *Brown v. Brown* (1996), 23 RFL (4th) 23 (Ont. Gen. Div.), the court ordered supervised exchanges due to the father's abuse of the mother during unsupervised exchanges. Although ordering that the exchanges be supervised in such cases may lessen the abuse to the mother and children, one would hope that the court would view the father's behavior as cause to reconsider the initial custody decision.

Evidentiary Issues in Custody and Access Cases

Although not necessary in every case, expert testimony on the effects of domestic violence on children is being introduced in many Canadian custody cases. The courts are becoming more sophisticated—understanding that custody assessors must be aware of the dynamics of domestic violence when it is an issue in a particular case. In fact, in *Haider v. Malach* (1999) SJ 315 (Sask. C.A.), the Saskatchewan court of appeal held that if an assessor lacks the necessary knowledge and experience in terms of domestic violence, his or her opinion should be heavily discounted. In that case, the appellate court reversed the trial court's order of custody to the abusive father and awarded custody to the mother, based partly on the trial court's inappropriate reliance on an expert who had little experience with domestic violence cases. Note that the expert may not need to have a particular degree: Sometimes the expert is a worker from the local battered women's shelter, as in *Hallett v. Hallett* (1993) OJ 3382 (Prov. Ct.).

In several recent cases, courts allowed assessors to give expert opinions regarding a child's fear of one of the parents due to domestic violence, resulting in awards of custody to the mother. In *Roda v. Roda* (2000) OJ 3786 (Ont. Sup. Ct.), and *Young v. Young* (1989) 19 RFL (3d) 227 (Ont. S.C.), access to the father was terminated due to the domestic violence and the children's and mother's fears of the father; in both cases, experts were involved. Similarly, in *Thind v. Thind* (1994) BCJ 1131 (S.C.) and *Blackburn v. Blackburn* (1995) OJ 2321 (Prov. Div.), experts testified about the negative effects of domestic violence on children—to show why fathers should not get custody. In *DJAW v. GDT* (2000) SJ 594 (Q.B.), an expert testified that abusive conduct cannot be changed by a brief class for abusers. In that case, however, the father also called a domestic violence expert as part of his successful motion to change primary custody from the mother to himself because the mother was now being abused by her new partner.

Parental Alienation Syndrome

As discussed in previous chapters, parents sometimes allege that the other parent has alienated the child from them. Although this, of course, could be the case, the high incidence of such allegations in domestic violence cases is grounds for examining such allegations very closely. It is quite possible that the children are alienated from a parent because they are afraid of him, having witnessed his emotional or physical abuse of the other parent. "From a societal perspective, the problem of male abusers denying or minimizing their abusive acts is a more pervasive and serious problem than the problem of women exaggerating or falsifying claims of abuse, or 'alienating' children from their fathers" (Bala, 2001). An example of such minimization is found in *Armstrong v. Kahn* (1997) 33 RFL (4th) 438 (Gen. Div.), in which the father allegedly abused both the mother and child after the parents separated. The father's response was to claim the mother was just trying to get him in trouble through false allegations. However, the court accepted expert testimony on domestic violence dynamics and denied the father access.

On the other hand, in *DS v. STS* (1997) OJ 4061 (Gen. Div.), the court found that the mother's allegations of abuse toward herself and the daughters were unfounded, and that she had alienated the daughters from their father. The court ordered structured access for the father, as well as counseling for everyone in the family; the parents were ordered to share legal custody. Although shared legal custody may be problematic in such cases, the court is to be commended for not switching custody to the father to punish the mother, as advocated by Richard Gardner, the primary proponent of "Parental Alienation Syndrome."[22]

Relocation and Childsnatching by Parent Within Canada

Of course, like other victims of domestic violence, Canadian battered women sometimes flee with their children within Canada, or petition courts for permission to relocate with the children. In one such trial court decision, the court stated that the mother's allegations of domestic violence by the father were not credible and were irrelevant to the custody decision. It also saw the father's juvenile criminal record as immaterial. In *Blackwell v. Burden* (1996) Ont. Ct. of Justice (Family Court), 1996 Ont. C. J. Lexis 782, the original custody order forbade the mother from moving the residence of the child away from London, Ontario, without giving notice to the father. However, without giving such notice to the father, she moved with the child to another city, quit her job, and became dependent on public assistance. (Note that although battered women are often forced to move and become dependent on public assistance, it is unclear in this case whether abuse was the basis for these actions.) She then moved back to London, and petitioned for permission to relocate to the new city. The court stated that it liked the father's girlfriend better than the mother's fiance, although it did not give any particular reasons for this preference. The court commented that the mother was unstable and immature and had frequently denied the father access. The court changed custody to the father, as he seemed more mature.

The Hague Convention Cases

As in the other countries included in this chapter, the response by Canadian courts to allegations of grave risk to children based on domestic violence toward their mothers has been mixed. For example, in *In RAH v. NJG* (1998) BCJ, the British Columbia court was presented with a situation in which an allegedly battered mother had fled to Canada from Texas, bringing her children with her. The court found that there was no grave risk, based on evidence that the mother had fabricated or exaggerated the abuse. It also found that the children's wishes to remain with the mother were probably due to her influence, and ordered the children's return to Texas.

The mother in *Pollastro v. Pollastro* (1999) 43 OR (3d) 458 (CA) also fled to Canada from the United States, and was initially granted temporary custody of the baby. However, she was also ordered to return the baby to the home jurisdiction for the permanent custody trial. The Canadian trial court called the relationship "stormy," and held that the home court could appropriately deal with the mother's safety concerns. The trial court was presented with evidence that while the mother was in the United States, the father called and screamed at her when she was at work, threatened her coworkers at their homes, disabled her car, followed her, and was very controlling. When the mother left the United States, she was covered with bruises and was emaciated. The father repeatedly called the mother's family in Canada after she left, and threatened that if she returned she would not be safe. He also said if he could not have the baby no one would, and that he would punish his wife by taking the one thing she loved more than life itself—her baby. The father, an admitted drug abuser, obtained a temporary custody order from a California court, not telling that court of the temporary custody order (in favor of the mother) from an Ontario court, which was already in effect.

The appellate court in Ontario took the evidence of the father's domestic violence, substance abuse, and lying to the court seriously, reversed the trial court decision, and found that there was a grave risk of physical and emotional harm to the baby based on the history of abuse to the mother by the father. It concluded that if the mother were to return to California, she would be in a dangerous situation, and the child would also be exposed to serious harm: "As a matter of common sense, returning a child to a violent environment places that child in an inherently intolerable situation."

A few months later, in *Finzio v. Soppio-Finzio* (1999) 46 OR (3d) 226 (CA), the same appellate court came to a different conclusion, based on very different facts. In this case, it did not believe there was a grave risk of harm to the children, and ordered their return to Italy. There had been only one alleged assault by the father on the mother, which occurred after the parties separated. The mother did not present medical evidence, although she claimed she had seen a doctor for her injuries. The children did not witness the assault, and continued to visit the father for another 6 weeks before the mother took them with her to Canada. The court also stated that there was no evidence that the Italian courts could not or would not protect the mother and children from the father.

Third Parties: New Partners, Grandparents

As in other countries, in some Canadian cases, the biological father has sought to change custody because the custodial mother is being abused by her new partner. In *DJAW v. GDT* (2000) SJ 594 (Q.B.), the court changed the previous sole custody order to joint custody, with the primary residence with the father. The court was concerned that the mother's "rationalization" of the abusive behavior of her new partner "gives no comfort that she will be able to extricate the children from risk of harm." See also *MacKay v. MacKay* (1995) NBJ 565 (Q.B. Fam. Div, in which custody was changed from the mother and her new partner to the father, due to verbal abuse and extensive corporal punishment of the child by the mother and her new partner.

Sometimes abusive fathers are given custody on the condition that they reside with their nonabusive mothers; this is essentially a custody award to the grandparent. Courts also may prefer biological parents over stepparents, even if the biological parent is abusive. In *Allen v. Allen* (1995) SJ 410 (Q.B.), the father was awarded custody of his daughter by a previous relationship in spite of evidence that he physically abused his new wife on several occasions. The abuse occurred in front of the child, resulting in a conviction. The father also regularly abused the new wife verbally. The court noted some sensitivity to the issue of domestic violence, stating that even though the father was taking an anger-management course as a condition of probation, "his problem is more serious than he has as yet admitted." However, it opined that the abuse may have been a relationship problem, which might stop when the marriage ended. Given that studies have shown that perpetrators are not likely to stop being abusive without long-term intervention and that domestic violence is rarely mutual, the court demonstrated a basic lack of understanding about the dynamics of domestic violence.

Termination of Parental Rights

As mentioned in Chapter 3, provincial child-protection legislation in Canada often specifically refers to domestic violence as a factor in finding that a child is in need of protection. Thus, child-protection issues based on abuse of the child's mother have arisen in many cases. Among these are *CAS of Sarnia v. DRS* (1995) OJ 4127 (Prov. Div.) and *Catholic CAS of Metro Toronto v. AD* (1993) OJ 3129 (Gen. Div.), in which spousal abuse was a factor in the protection proceedings.

As in the United States, Canadian courts may use a concern for children to terminate the parental rights of battered mothers. Child-protection agencies filed petitions in cases in which battered mothers let the abuser return in *CAS of Peel v. PT* (1995) OJ 103 (Prov Ct) and *CAS of Haldimand-Norfolk v. DC* (1996) OJ 3471 (Ont. Gen. Div.). Similarly, in *New Brunswick (Minister of Health and Community Services) v. BL* (2000) NBJ 67 (N.B.Q.B) and *Nova Scotia (Minister of Community Services) v. Z(S)* (1999) 5 RFL (5th) 435 (N.S.C.A.), the mother's failure to leave an abusive relationship was grounds for making the child a permanent ward of the court. In other cases, such as *CAS Ottawa-Carleton v. RL* (1996) OJ 746 (Prov. Ct.), the parental rights of both parents were terminated due to allegations of mutual parental abuse, combined with abuse or neglect of the children. One wonders if the outcomes of any of these cases would have been different if the mothers had been offered supportive services addressing the violence and other problems in their lives.

Notably, there were no Canadian cases found in which battered women faced criminal charges for "failing to protect" their children from abusive partners. This appears to be a significant difference between how Canadian and U.S. courts handle child-protection cases. There were also no Canadian cases found in which someone's parental rights were terminated for having killed the coparent. This may be because the homicide rate in Canada is so much lower than it is in the United States.

❖ AUSTRALIA

Historical Overview

Domestic violence is often raised as an issue in child-custody and access cases in Australia. One study found that such allegations occurred in 24% of the cases heard in 1990 throughout the country; 22% alleged violence against the wife by the husband and 2% alleged violence against the mother by a new partner. There were no allegations of violence by the wife against the husband (see Parkinson, 1995). The same commentator noted that as of 1995, "the way in which domestic violence is relevant to custody and access decision-making has not yet been clearly established." Although the Family Law Amendments of 1995 sought to clarify this standard, and appellate courts now often cite those amendments, it appears that decisions made pretrial or by trial courts still reflect a fundamental tension regarding whether domestic violence is an important factor.

In a custody decision that was typical until recently, an older Australian case demonstrates the basic lack of understanding of family courts concerning the effect of domestic violence. In that case, *Heidt v. Heidt* (1976) 1 Fam L R 11576, 11 ALR 594, the court seems to have believed the mother's evidence concerning the father's domestic violence toward her, but saw this violence as irrelevant to the custody decision. The court actually stated, "in assessing his potential as a custodial parent I have largely disregarded his behaviour as a husband." The three older children were living with the father, and the mother had access during the weekends. The court transferred custody to the mother, and gave the father access, stating that even though there was no evidence that the father was physically abusive to the children, he seemed interested in them mostly either to get the mother to return to him or "for some financial reason." The court also noted that the mother's "instability" (a suicide attempt) had been caused by the father's ill treatment of her, and that it appeared that the father had committed adultery with another woman while the spouses were still living together. The court declined the mother's request for an injunction (protective order) against the father, stating, "If however, the generous access which I envisage being granted to the husband is to work, relationships between the parties will have to be rebuilt. To assist in this, it may be preferable for the husband to give an undertaking on oath as to nonmolestation of his wife rather than have the heavy hand of an injunction lie against him."

This statement is very troubling for several reasons. First, the court did not even consider the possibility that a third party could be a go-between in terms of taking the children from one parent to the other, to prevent more abuse by the father. Second, the court seemed to believe that the father's promise not to molest his wife would stop him from doing so, a very naive point of view. Third, the court's characterization of an injunction as "heavy-handed" indicates that the court did not take seriously the history of domestic violence or the wife's request for help in stopping it. See also *In the Marriage of Chandler* (1981) 6 Fam L R 736; FLC 91-008, a similar case where the court ordered joint custody despite allegations of domestic violence by the husband, ruling that such allegations were irrelevant to the issue of custody.

In the 1980s, this attitude began to change, and domestic violence received increasing attention in custody decisions.[23] Of course, as we have seen in the countries previously discussed, awareness of the effect of domestic violence on children can result in mothers losing custody to fathers when the mother becomes involved with a violent boyfriend. See, for example, *In the Marriage of Jaeger* (1994) 18 Fam L R 126; FLC 92-492, in which custody to the mother was reversed and a new trial ordered because evidence of significant injuries suffered by the mother and inflicted by her new partner had been excluded.

Cases decided under the latest statutes in Australia demonstrate mixed, but overall promising, results. As noted in the previous chapter, a major legislative amendment affecting Part VII of the Family Law Act was enacted in 1995 and came into force in June 1996. The amendment contained somewhat contradictory provisions, as it provided for the child's right to contact with both parents and also for serious consideration of any history of domestic violence. Courts have taken differing approaches in resolving this conflict, as is discussed in the following section.

Custody

Increasingly, reported cases show that Australian courts consider domestic violence by one parent toward the other to be relevant to custody decisions. For example, in *Holswich v. O'Farrell* (1996/1997) 21

Fam L R 210; (1997) FLC 83,916 (& 92-735), the mother alleged that the father assaulted her while she was pregnant and also stalked her. The trial court stated that it did not fully believe the mother's allegations, and issued an interim order that the father have "reasonable" access, "as agreed between the parties." However, after trial, the court ordered only very limited and supervised contact with the child, which was upheld on appeal. Both the trial and appellate courts relied on the new statutory provisions as part of the best interests of the child analysis. The trial court stated, "It is important for children to know both parents whether they be angels or sinners." The appellate court agreed with the very limited contact, because the statute provides that the child has a right to contact with both parents "except when it is or would be contrary to a child's best interests."

In *Blanch v. Blanch* (1998/1999) Fam LR 325; (1999) FLC 85,738 (& 92-837), the court faced the dilemma of both the father (the mother's ex-spouse) and the mother's new boyfriend being abusive. Against the recommendation of the children's representative, the trial court awarded the father custody. This was due in part to the father's having been the primary caretaker since separation; he and the children had been living with his own mother. The court was also concerned about the violent history of the wife's new boyfriend and, thus, whether the father would be allowed any access.

In reversing and remanding the case to another trial judge, the appellate court criticized the trial court for not making clear findings as to whether domestic violence had, in fact, occurred, and how it reached that conclusion. It also disagreed that the history of abuse was relatively equal between the parties, and that "the husband's violence towards the wife was a product of the marital relationship rather than of the husband's personality." It held that domestic violence is an important factor in cases relating to parenting orders. It also stated that this is partly due to the risk to the children's safety, but more particularly because of the risk to their emotional development. The appellate court cited the new amendments to the Family Law Act, which make very clear the importance of domestic violence as a factor for consideration. A concurring judge noted that the trial judge focused too much on the physical abuse, and discounted the more serious allegations of ongoing emotional abuse toward the wife, and destruction of property by the husband. Showing a sophisticated understanding of the potential effects of domestic violence on children, this judge emphasized the potential threat to the emotional development of the children, the possibility of long-term poor self-esteem and lack of self-confidence, and the likelihood that children, when raised by a batterer, would also use violence in their future relationships. See also *Crawford v. Crawford* (1999) FLC 92-837, in which domestic violence also influenced the outcome of the custody decision.

An unusual legal issue was presented in *In the Marriage of A* (1998) 22 Fam L R 756 sub nom *A v. A* (1998) FLC 84,985. The court held that the children had a right to be informed of their mother's claim she had been abused by their father, and the right to discuss this claim.

Access

Australian courts are also showing increasing concern about the impact of domestic violence in access decisions. In several cases, they have either denied or cut off access due to the effect of the domestic violence on both the custodial parent and the children. The impact on the mother seems to be given more importance in the Australian courts than in the courts of the other three countries discussed in this chapter.

For example, *Re Andrew* (1996) FLC 83,195 (& 92-692) held that an appropriate consideration in a domestic violence case is the effect of an access order on the custodial parent. In this case, the father had told the mother that he was suicidal, then came to her house and grabbed her around the neck. Their ensuing fight was witnessed by the son. The same day the father had tied a tie around the child's neck, later claiming he was showing the boy how to knot a tie. The father was convicted of assault on the mother. Even though the court was not convinced that the child's safety was in danger, supervised access was ordered, because the custodial parent was genuinely afraid for the safety of herself and the child.

Upon review a few months later, the court's dilemma was that although supervised access seemed beneficial to the boy, the father felt he could not continue to pay $50 per visit. There was no supervised access center in the area at the time. The court terminated access until such a center was established, but allowed the father to continue to contact the boy through letters and phone calls, and ordered the mother to encourage the boy to respond. It also ordered her to keep the father apprised of important developments in the boy's life, and to arrange for counselling for the boy. The appellate court upheld this decision, but suggested that supervised access could begin again when the father could arrange for another professional supervisor, rather than waiting for an access center to open. This case reinforces the great need for low-cost supervised access centers, or, perhaps, video conferencing in lieu of personal access, in all countries.

In some cases, the courts have stated that the custodial parent should not have veto power over the other parent's access, but the reasons the custodial parent is concerned for the child's safety and his or her own must be given consideration.[24] A commentator suggests that although it is admirable that the court recognizes the potential impact of access on the mother's parenting, "the onus of proof, however, ought to be on the father to show the benefits of access despite the mother's fears rather than for her to demonstrate that her reasonable fears would have a detrimental impact upon her parenting capacity" (Parkinson, 1995, p. 56).

Sometimes custodial battered mothers' opposition to access is seen as inappropriate. In a passage reminiscent of allegations of Parental Alienation Syndrome, the court in *N and S* (1996) FLC 92-655, commented: "In many cases this problem arises because the custodial parent quite irrationally and wrongly creates such difficulties about access that its continuance has a demonstrable detrimental effect upon the child." The problem was resolved by using a best interests of the child analysis, rather than resorting to punishment of the custodial parent. "The matter is to be determined having regard to the welfare of the child, not by considerations of either sympathy for the innocent noncustodial parent or feelings of frustration or annoyance with the custodial parent." The court left open the option of changing custody to the formerly noncustodial parent, with access to the formerly custodial parent.

In some cases, the court decides that the best long-term solution is to terminate access due to the father's abuse of the mother and children. For example, in *M v. M* (2000) FLC 93-006; (1998) Fam CA 1742, the father had been convicted of abusing the wife and her young son (his stepson) and had bragged about using violence with many people. The parents had two young children together, in addition to the wife's stepson. The father frequently threatened to kill his wife and children; fought with strangers, police officers, lawyers, and others; and was extremely controlling of everyone around him. On cross-examination, he never took responsibility for the violence: He admitted being violent, but claimed this was only in self-defense or when he had to hit his wife to get her to properly supervise the children. His young stepson had already begun showing violent tendencies toward the mother and the younger sister.

Past orders had included custody of the two younger children to the father with access to the mother. At times the access was, in effect, joint physical custody, and, not surprisingly, had not worked. At the time of trial, the mother was the custodial parent, and the father sought contact 1 or 2 days a week. The court held that a permanent separation from the father was needed, because there was no possibility of a worthwhile relationship with him. The court also stated that the father was a danger to the children and was also likely to undermine the mother's care of them. The court referred to the mother as "a parent who is already very vulnerable and having problems coping." It ordered contact supervised by a professional at the court counseling service over a 12-month period to facilitate separation from the father. This period would also give the father a final chance to recognize his problem and undertake successful therapy, which the court regarded as highly unlikely but possible. The mother was given the sole right to make decisions regarding the parties' children. The court ordered the mother not to move outside the local area during this period (in case the father reformed) to cooperate with the Department of Community Services, and to continue her own counseling. Finally, it prohibited the father from filing any proceedings for contact or alleging sexual abuse of the children within the next 3 years, except by permission of the court. In effect, this father was found to be a vexatious litigant, having used the legal system to continue abusing his ex-partner and the children.

In spite of the clear trend in reported decisions toward giving domestic violence significant weight in custody and access decisions, researchers commenting on developments since the 1995 amendments went into effect raise alarming concerns. One commentator states that "no fault" divorce has come to mean that domestic violence is irrelevant (Graycar, 1995).

Two other commentators observe: "Although the new family violence provisions have allegedly made a big impact on the practices and decision-making of the court, it also appears that structural systemic factors may prevent violence issues from being properly dealt with in the many cases that are not litigated" (Dewar & Parker, 1999, p. 107).

Among these systemic factors, they point to the decline in funding for free legal services for indigent parents, resulting in a large increase of parties forced to represent themselves. This, in turn, leads to fewer cases coming to the attention of judges, and more cases resolved pretrial. The commentators refer to this trend as the "horizontalization of law," by which they mean what lawyers tell clients and each other, what clients and mediators discuss, and what clients tell each other about the standards and what to expect. All these nonjudicial discussions may be based on incorrect information and may shape client expectations and behavior (Dewar & Parker, 1999).

The same commentators argue that the new model being developed outside the courtroom in Australia gives the nonresident parent, usually the father, more power, because it requires both parents to consult on virtually every decision. In some cases, fathers will deliberately use this power to continue to control their former partners (Dewar & Parker, 1999). Many of these arrangements, which may be sanctioned at an interim (pretrial) hearing, would not withstand the closer scrutiny of trial and appeal, but never reach those stages. According to the commentators, this new model is based on an over-emphasis on two parts of the new Family Law Amendments: the provision that each child has "a right to contact" with both parents and the assumption that parental responsibility is to be shared by both parents irrespective of their separation. The commentators note that the almost exclusive focus on these provisions has resulted in restrictions on many custodial parents' ability to relocate, and has cut down on no-contact orders, even though other provisions in the Act stress the importance of domestic violence as a custody and access factor. The commentators conclude that "women are the big losers of the changes" (Dewar & Parker, 1999, p. 112).

These same concerns are voiced in an extensive Interim Report released in April 1999, titled *The Family Law Reform Act 1995: Can Changing Legislation Change Legal Culture, Legal Practice and Community Expectations?* The authors, Helen Rhoades, Reg Graycar, and Margaret Harrison, note that attorneys now caution battered women that "you can move if you have a new husband or a job to go to, but not if you want to get away from a violent ex-husband" (Rhoades, Graycar, & Harrison, 1999, p. 70). Perhaps most alarming was the finding that many attorneys and judges were unaware of the domestic violence provisions of the amendments. Similar to Graycar's comments in 1995, some of the attorneys surveyed after the reforms went into effect stated that the clock has been turned back 10 years, so that domestic violence is now seen as irrelevant in custody decisions. In the most extreme case cited, even though the father had actually been convicted of assaulting the mother during contact with the children, contact was not cut off (Rhoades et al., 1999).

Furthermore, the Interim Report found that the average time from filing to a court hearing now exceeds 70 weeks in about half the family law cases in Australia. This leads to a greater reliance on interim orders. Prereform, judges tended to err on the side of caution at the interim stage, suspending contact in many domestic violence cases until trial; postreform, they are more likely to order contact until trial, then terminate contact once they find it is not in the best interests of the child.

These studies indicate that there is a need for more low-cost or free Australian attorneys working on family law cases, and also for more speedy access to the courts, especially in domestic violence cases. In addition, legal aid needs to be provided specifically to victims of domestic violence; the Interim Report found that free aid is provided to fathers who want contact but not to mothers who want to cut it off due to abuse (Rhoades et al., 1999).

The Hague Convention Cases

Australian courts have also been dealing with international custody cases under the Hague Convention on International Child Abduction. As in the Hague cases discussed earlier in this chapter, in the five reported cases in Australia in which domestic violence was alleged as possible grounds for a finding of grave risk to the child, it was the mother who was allegedly the victim of the father's abuse. There are two striking and interrelated trends shown in these five cases.

The first trend is the courts' practice of always relying only on affidavits (often from one party only) as opposed to holding an evidentiary hearing. This seems to be because the Australian courts interpret the Hague Convention as requiring that the matter be decided very quickly. (See, for example, the discussion of the need for a quick resolution in *Gsponer v. Johnstone* [1989]) 12 Fam L R 755, which appears to be the first in this line of cases.) Note that courts in the other countries previously discussed have not interpreted the Convention in this way, and often quickly hold evidentiary hearings.

The second trend in these Australian cases is the appellate courts' refusal in every case to find that there was a grave risk of danger to the child—should the child be returned to the home country. This occurs despite serious allegations of domestic violence and child abuse. In *Murray v. Director of Family Services* (1993) 16 Fam L R 982, the wife alleged a history of assaults and provided photographs of her injuries; the husband maintained an extensive weapons collection and was a member in a gang. Similarly, the judge in *Cooper v. Casey* (1995) FLC 92-575 referred to the wife's affidavits of abuse as "most chilling in its detail." However, no grave risk was found in either case.

It appears that the refusal of the Australian courts to ever find a grave risk of danger to the child is based on their never holding an evidentiary hearing in this type of case. Thus, each court states that it cannot really tell what the level of danger is, because it only has affidavits before it. For example, in the *Murray* case, the appellate court, agreeing with the trial court, stated, "His Honour [the trial court judge] commented that it was not possible to determine the veracity of these allegations and that most of the evidence in relation to them would only be available in New Zealand."

It also appears that the Australian courts automatically assume that if the parents have access to a court in the home country, with or without attorneys, and if the home country makes custody decisions based on the best interest of the child, there will never be a grave risk of danger to the child because the home country court will adequately protect him or her. This assumption is very naive. For one thing, it assumes that the perpetrators will obey court orders in the home country, which many perpetrators of domestic violence refuse to do.

The Australian courts also sometimes show a lack of understanding of the danger facing these mothers and children. For example, in the *Cooper* case, even though the mother had a California restraining order when she fled with the children to Australia, and had raised very serious allegations of violence, the Australian court ordered the mother to inform the father of her and the children's whereabouts as soon as they returned to the United States. Complying with this order could very well put her and the children in serious danger.

In several of these cases, mothers were ordered to return with the children to their home countries, even if they would be unrepresented there. Australian appellate courts appear to believe that an unrepresented battered parent will be able to adequately present the relevant law and evidence in the custody case, holding her own against the perpetrator and his attorney (if he hires one). This is highly unlikely, especially if there is a long history of controlling behavior by the batterer.

At the same time, in several of these cases, the appellate judges did express concerns about the fact that the home country currently had no obligation to see that the child is safe (*Cooper v. Casey* (1995), *McOwan v. McOwan* (1994), 17 Fam L R 337, and *Department of Families, Youth, and Community Care v. Bennett* (2000) Fam CA 253). In *Cooper*, one of the judges explicitly urged the creation of a new standard, under which the home country would "accept a positive obligation for the welfare of the child," especially in cases where there were allegations of domestic violence or child abuse. In *McOwan*, the court stated that such an obligation could include free legal assistance if the fleeing parent has no funds—often the case with battered mothers: "There is however no mechanism within the Convention that enables the Contracting State which is ordering the return of the children, to ensure that the State to where the children are returned actually provides the mechanism to enable a proper hearing to take place. This is not necessarily limited to the provision of a forum for the hearing of the dispute. It may also require the provision of appropriate legal representation." Similarly, in *Cooper*, the wife had legal assistance in Australia but would be forced to represent herself when she and the children returned to the United States. In spite of such expressions of concern, however, the Australian courts ordered these unrepresented victims of domestic violence to take their children back to the home country, finding that there was no grave risk to the children.

The most recent of the cases, *Bennett*, was the only case in which the trial court found that ordering the child to be returned to the home country (England) would create an intolerable situation for the child. This was based on the mother's inability to advocate for herself and the child in a custody battle conducted far away from the mother's family, due to her serious depression. However, this decision was reversed by the appellate court. Notably, the domestic violence allegations became buried so deep in the appellate decision that they effectively disappeared. Even though the abuse by the husband was the underlying cause of the wife's depression and anxiety, for which she was seeing an Australian psychiatrist, the appellate court reduced the issue to whether the wife could travel. It concluded that because there were also psychiatrists in England, there was no reason that she and the child could not go back. In the process, the court dismissed the evidence that the wife's only source of emotional or financial support was her family in Australia. Further, even though the court knew the wife had no income, the court stated, "There was no evidence placed before the Court to indicate that it would be impossible for the wife to live in England apart from the husband." Thus, the court turned a blind eye to the likelihood that the wife might be forced to live with her abusive husband if she and the child were ordered to return to England, displaying a troublesome disregard for the practical realities of the lives of victims and children in domestic violence.

❖ CONCLUSION

Overall, the cases reviewed in this chapter indicate that courts are increasingly aware of the implications of domestic violence when making custody and visitation decisions. However, they also demonstrate that many courts, especially at the trial level, are still denying or minimizing the impact of domestic violence on children and the potential for further abuse after the parents have separated. Joint custody awards to batterers and their former victims, "generous access" or "reasonable visitation" awards, and even awards of sole custody to batterers are still being made. The push for frequent contact between the child and both parents is strong in many places, and sometimes prevails even in cases with a significant history of domestic violence.

In the United States, victims of domestic violence too frequently have their children taken away from them by the juvenile family courts. This also appears to be occurring in New Zealand. In many cases, this happens not because the mothers themselves abused the children, but because the mothers' abusive boyfriends or husbands committed these crimes in front of the children, and the mothers "failed to protect" the children from this exposure. In the court's attempt to protect children, many children are actually revictimized by being cut off from a nonoffending parent.

In the area of international custody decisions, Hague Convention cases from all four countries are similarly mixed in their understanding of the dynamics of domestic violence and its impact on children. Although some cases show a sophisticated approach to the problem, in many cases, courts do not fully explore the question of "grave risk" to the children, summarily sending them back to the country where the abuser lives and hoping that court-ordered "undertakings," including the abuser's promising to provide a safe place for the mother and children to stay and not harm them, will hold true. Courts often assume that battered mothers will be able to proceed fairly in the home country's custody courts—even if the mother has no money to hire an attorney—and discount the need in some cases for the victimized mother to have the support of her family in the country to which she has fled. Although the Hague Convention does not address the best interests of the child, the procedural decisions can have a significant impact on the eventual outcome of the custody case.

NOTES

1. The best interests of the child is the basic standard governing custody decisions in all U.S. jurisdictions. Its interpretation leaves a great deal up to the discretion of the trial court judge, who may or may not see this standard as including consideration of abuse by one of the parents toward an intimate partner.

2. Examples of this are found in *Brainerd v. Brainerd* (Iowa App. 1994), 523 N.W.2d 611, *R.H. v. B.F.* (Mass. App. 1995), 653 N.E.2d 195, *Peters v. Blue* (N.Y. Fam. Ct. 1997), 661 N.Y.S.2d 722, and *Keesee v. Keesee* (Fla/ Dist. Ct. App. 1996), 675 So.2d 655.

3. These include *Bruner v. Jaeger* (N.D. 1995), 534 N.W.2d 825, *Krank v. Krank* (N.D. 1996), 541 N.W.2d 714, *Ternes v. Ternes* (N.D. 1996), 555 N.W.2d 355, *Zuger v. Zuger* (N.D. 1997), 563 N.W.2d 804, and *Huesers v. Huesers* (N.DE. 1997), 560 N.W.2d 219.

4. See also *Morrison v. Morrison v. Morrison* (La. App. 1997), 699 So.2d 1124, *Lovcik v. Ellingson* (N.D. 1997), 569 N.W.2d 697, *Kahn v. Kahn* (N.Y. App. 1997), 654 N.Y.S.2d 34, and *Berg v. Berg* (N.D. 2000), 606 N.W.2d 895 (mother found to be batterer of father).

5. Examples of courts taking domestic violence into account in permitting such relocation out of state are found in *Carter v. Carter* (Mo. App. 1997), 940 S.W.2d 12, *In re Marriage of Williams* (Iowa Ct. App. 1998), 589 N.W.2d 759, *Hayes v. Gallagher* (Nev. 1999), 972 P.2d 1138, and *O'Neill v. Stone* (Fla. Dist. Ct. App. 1998), 721 So.2d 393.

6. See, for example, *Barkaloff v. Woodward* (Cal. Appl. 1996), 47 Cal. App. 4th 393 ([...]), *Matter of CM (MM)* (N.Y. Fam. Ct. 1998), 672 N.Y.S.2d 1012 ([...]), *Benzon v. Sosa* (N.Y. App. 1997), 663 N.Y.S.2d 938 (maternal grandmother awarded custody of children when mother died accidentally, due in part to father's abuse of mother).

7. See *In the Matter of the Appeal in Maricopa County Juv. Action No. JD-6123* (Ariz. App. 1997), 956 P.2d 511, *In re Sylvia R. et al.* (Cal. App. 1997), 55 Cal. App. 4th 559, *In re Heather A.* (Cal. App. 1996), 52 Cal. App. 2000), 80 Cal. App. 4th 470.

8. See *In re Sabrina N.* (Cal. App. 1998), 60 Cal. App. 4th 996.

9. See *In the Interest of DJS et al.* (Fla. App. 1990), 563 So.2d 655, and *In the Matter of Marquise EE* (N.Y. App. Div. 1999), 257 A.D.2d 699 (battered mother also held in contempt and given 6-month suspended jail sentence).

10. See *In re G.V.* (Ill. App. 1997), 685 N.E.2d 406, and *Smith v. Smith* (Nev. 1996), 927 P.2d 14.

11. See *In the Interest of HLT* (Ga. App. 1982), 298 S.E.2d 33, *In re Tracy Ann Lutgen* (Ill. App. 1988), 532 N.E.2d 976, and *Bartasavich v. Mitchell* (Pa. Super. 1984), 471 A.2d 833.

12. See *In re CMJ et al.* (Ill. App. 1996), 663 N.E.2d 498, *In the Matter of Sara R* (N.M. 1997), 945 P.2d 76, *In re AWJ* (Ill. App. Ct. 2000), 736 N.E.2d 716, *In re Edgar O.* (Cal. Ct. of App. 2000), 84 Cal. App. 4th 13, and *In re Scott JJ* (Matthew HH v. Vincent JJ) 2001 WL 112221 (N.Y. App. Div. 2001).

13. See also *Molloy v. Molloy* (1991) Ont Ct of Jus, 1991 Ont. C. J. Lexis 1509 (allegations of domestic violence, if true, relevant to father's ability to parent; trial court should be presented with all relevant evidence); *Carlson v. Carlson* (1991) BC Ct of App, 1991 DLR Lexis 1803, 81 DLR4th 185 (custody to father reversed, partly due to counsellor's having totally discounted father's physical abuse of mother and child and his abducting child); *Stewart v. Mix* (1995) BCJ 2414 (S.C.) (court rejected assessor's recommendation that father have custody, noting father's history of violent temper and jealousy); *Pare v. Pare* (1993) SJ 511 (Q.B.) (mother awarded sole custody due to physical and mental abuse by father); *Blackburn v. Blackburn* (1995) OJ 2321 (Prov Ct) (mother awarded custody not only because of the abuse from the father, but also because it was likely that the father would undermine access and the children's meaningful relationship with the mother); *Pierce v. Van Loon* (1997) (Supreme Court of British Columbia, a trial court) (father's temper tantrums seen as psychological abuse; however court criticized mother for forming friendships with other formerly battered women); *KHP v. RP (Plank v. Plank)* (1997), (Supreme Court of British Columbia) (court did not believe mother's allegations of domestic violence generally, but awarded her custody; father not sincerely interested in custody); *Tittemore v. Tittemore* (1996) BCJ 238 (S.C.) (mother awarded sole custody, liberal access to father; however, pick up and drop off is at mother's residence which, given father's history, almost certainly will result in further abuse).

14. See, for example, *Boothby v. Boothby* (1996) OJ 4346 (Prov. Div.) (joint custody awarded in spite of history of emotional abuse and controlling behavior by father); Smith v. Smith (1997) SJ 765 (Q.B.) (joint custody ordered in spite of finding that husband had assaulted wife, court concerned that wife would try to keep father from children); Mbaruk v. Mbaruk (1996, Supreme Court of B.C.) (joint custody, primary residence with father in spite of history of father abusing mother and dismissing her role in children's lives).

15. Hallett v. Hallett (1993) OJ 3382 (Prov. Ct.), DEC v. DTG (1997) OJ 1976 (Gen. Div.) and TNL v. BCM (1996) BCJ 2743 (Prov. Ct.).

16. *DM v. LM* (1993) OJ 1973 (Ont. Prov. Ct.) (primary residence with mother, her condition under control from drug treatment).

17. See, for example, *Pereira v. Pereira* (1995) BCJ 2151 (S.C.) (husband attempted to arrange for wife's murder after separation).

18. See, for example, *Rasalingam v. Rasalingam* (1991) OJ 1241 (Prov. Ct.), *Bolton v. Bolton* (1995) SJ 64 (Q.B.), *DiMeco v. DiMeco* (1995) OJ 3650 (U.F.C.), and *Roda v. Roda* (2000) OJ 3786 (Ont. Sup. Ct.).

19. See, for example, *BPM v. BLDEM*, 1992 Ont Ct of App, 97 DLR4th 437 (1992 DLR Lexis 2289) (dissent argued in favor of continuing supervised access, due to domestic violence and stalking in past); *Abdo v. Abdo* (1993) Nova Scotia Ct of App, 1993 DLR Lexis 1502, 109 DLR 4th 78 (supervised access cut off, due to father's inappropriate behavior and its effect on mother); *PA v. FA* (1997, Supreme Court of British Columbia) (no access until father enrolled in counselling and took responsibility for having abused mother and children; any future access up to children); *Pavao v. Pavao* (2000) OJ 1010 (Ct. Just.) (supervised access terminated; father's access limited to writing and sending presents to child); *Parker v. Hall* (1996) OJ 756 (Ont. Prov. Ct.); *Alexander v. Creary* (1995) 14 RFL (4th) 311 (Ont. Prov. Ct.); *Matheson v. Sabourin* (1994) OJ 991 (Prov. Ct.) (preseparation abuse by father continued after separation); *Lacaille v. Manger* (1994) OJ 2880 (Prov. Div.); and *CD v. JB* (1996) AQ 181 (supervised access terminated due to abusive conduct, failure to regularly visit, or failure to complete court-ordered program).

20. See, for example, *DeSilva v. Giggey* (1996) NBJ 133 (Q.B.), and *Drummond v. Drummond* (1995) BCJ 1560 (S.C.).

21. See, for example, *Sekhri v. Mahli* (1993) 112 Sask.R. 253 (U.F.C.) (mother grossly exaggerated abuse, which made daughter believe father would kill her; initial access supervised; counselling for mother and daughter, psychiatric assessment of father ordered); *Zahr v. Zahr* (1994) 24 Alta LR (3d) 274 (Q.B.) (supervised access ordered due to father's threats to abduct child to another country, child's witnessing violence toward mother, child's not having seen father for 2 years); *Fullerton v. Fullerton* (1994) 7 RFL(4th) 272 (N.B. Fam. Div.) (supervised exchange ordered when father assaulted mother during pick up of children; father ordered to abstain from drugs, alcohol, and displays of violence or threats in presence of children); *H.H. v. H.C.* (2002) ABQB 426 (supervised access ordered in light of serious history of physical attacks by husband against wife and other abuse; wife had opposed all access due to danger).

22. See also *Morrison v. Senko* (1997) SJ 113 (Sask. Q. B.) (allegations of "Parental Alienation Syndrome").

23. See *M v. M* (1988) 166 CLR 69; 12 Fam L R 606; (1988) FLC 91-979 (parent's tendency to be violent unacceptable risk to well-being of child); *In the Marriage of Homsy* (1993) 115 FL 235 sub nom Homsy v. Yassa 17 Fam L R 299 (1994) FLC 80,606 (father pled guilty to manslaughter of mother, denied supervised access with son when released); *In the Marriage of JG and BG* (1994) 18 Fam. L. R. 255; FLC 92-515 (exposure to family violence detrimental to children, especially when associated with pattern of dominance: "It is quite wrong to assume that violence can be relevant only if it is directed at the children or takes place in their presence."); and *Patsalou and Patsalou* (1995) FLC 92-580 (batterers unsuitable custodial parents; court cites literature addressing this).

24. See *B and B* (1993) FLC 92-357; *Grant and Grant* (1994) FLC 92-506; *Sedgley v. Sedgley* (1995) FLC 92-623; and *Irvine* (1995) FLC 92-624 (importance of impact of access on custodial battered mother's ability to care for child when genuinely afraid for herself and child).

5

A Framework for Action by Courts and Communities to Recognize the Plight of Abused Victims and Their Children After Separation

The preceding chapters have outlined how domestic violence has been overlooked or minimized by legal and mental health services responding to child-custody disputes. Studies based on domestic violence survivors' accounts of their dealings with the justice system and various community services suggest that much work is required to adequately support abused women and their children (Graham-Bermann & Edleson, 2001). Many survivors speak of their revictimization by the very service systems designed to protect them. Rather than safety and healing from traumatic events, these survivors report ongoing dangers in their lives from ex-partners, and never-ending litigation that drains their financial and emotional resources.

Most surveys of domestic violence survivors and research on child-custody disputes reveal consistent themes on the best remedies to make courts and communities more responsive to their problems. These remedies include legislation, training, policy development, resource development, and coordination of services. This chapter addresses each of these themes with reference to promising innovations.

❖ LEGISLATION

Legislation is vital to guide judges in assessing and managing complex custody disputes that involve histories of domestic violence. Good legislation has an impact beyond the courtroom in educating parents and service providers that domestic violence is harmful to both victims and children exposed to the violence. The public becomes more aware that being a good parent includes respectful and nonviolent behavior toward the other parent, as well as toward the children. For example, legislation in New York clearly indicates that exposure to domestic violence is harmful to children and needs to be given significant weight in the determination of child custody:

> The legislature finds and declares that there has been a growing recognition across the country that domestic violence should be a weighty consideration in custody and visitation cases. The legislature recognizes the wealth of research demonstrating the effects of domestic violence on children, even when the children have been neither physically abused themselves nor witnesses to the violence. Studies indicate that children raised in a violent home experience shock, fear, and guilt and suffer anxiety, depression, low self-esteem, and developmental and socialization difficulties. Additionally, children raised by a violent parent face increased risk of abuse. A high correlation has been found between spouse and child abuse. (Susser, 2001, p. 200)

In Chapter 3, a Model Code was outlined, which was developed by the National Council of Juvenile and Family Court Judges (NCJFCJ) after years of study by a blue ribbon panel of judges, lawyers, and court-related service providers (National Council of Juvenile & Family

Court Judges, 1994). The key elements in the custody and visitation sections of the model code are the presumption that domestic violence perpetrators should not have sole or joint custody, and that there should be careful consideration of safety plans and supervised visitation in collaboration with other community programs. As discussed in Chapter 3, U.S. states have varied as to the degree of implementation of the Model Code. In Canada, legislation has been almost silent on domestic violence, but current judgments imply a clear recognition of the issue. In New Zealand, legislation has explicitly addressed the harmful effects of domestic violence on children and the need for thoughtful safety planning, as well as intervention programs for batterers (see Geffner et al., 2000, for a full review).

The essential elements for effective legislation to address domestic violence in child-custody laws include the following:

- Domestic violence must be assessed as a factor.
- Domestic violence should be given significant weight when there is evidence of significant physical, sexual, and/or psychological abuse of one parent by the other parent.
- The court must be able to order limited supervised visitation as well as appropriate rehabilitation programs for domestic violence offenders.
- The court should require evidence only on balance of probability to make domestic violence findings, rather than proof from criminal proceedings beyond a reasonable doubt, in light of the fact that domestic violence remains a well-hidden crime.
- Legislation must include a presumption against a perpetrator of domestic violence having either sole or joint custody.
- Legislation must include a presumption that victims/survivors of domestic violence will not be coerced in any fashion into mediation or parent-education programs with their abuser.

Legislatures need to pass laws creating government-sponsored confidential address programs so victims can relocate safely within the same community, even if the children continue to have access to the other parent. There needs to be clear rules about the interaction between protective orders and custody/access orders so the latter do not conflict with the former. It is not uncommon to have criminal and civil courts make orders that contradict each other due to a lack of information sharing and coordination of services.

For legislative reform to occur, politicians and lawmakers need to be educated about the relevance of domestic violence in the determination of child-custody and visitation decisions. They need to be educated about the exaggerated claims of fathers' rights groups—that most domestic violence allegations are false and that disputes could be avoided by replacing "custody" with "shared parenting plans." For legislators to gain the clearest understanding, however, the issue must be presented through the eyes of children living with domestic violence, rather than through the competing claims of fathers' rights groups and domestic violence advocates.

❖ TRAINING

Training is essential for an effective community response to domestic violence. At a minimum, training should consist of mandatory domestic violence education for attorneys, judges, and other players in the legal system. Education should not be limited to professionals, but should include everyone involved; the education should provide clear information about actual legal standards in the various settings, so parents do not enter into inappropriate and dangerous agreements based on misinformation and hearsay.

Ideally, training should raise awareness of domestic violence and develop specific skills for individual professionals, such as assessment of lethality, safety planning, and referrals to appropriate community services. In child-custody disputes involving domestic violence, one hopes that all professionals in contact with the family will have the necessary training to assist individual family members and document their concerns. Training is especially critical for custody evaluators and assessors, family law lawyers, and judges involved in these matters.

The extent to which training is essential is reflected in recent California legislation that requires custody evaluators to have at least 16 hours of training in domestic violence before undertaking the complex work of assessment. Under Rule 1257.7, "Domestic Violence Training Standards for Court-Appointed Child Custody Investigators and Evaluators" (California Family Law: Special Rules for Trial

Courts), evaluators must complete an initial 12 hours of classroom instruction and 4 hours of "community resource networking to acquaint the evaluator with domestic violence resources in the geographical communities where the families being evaluated may reside." The classroom training covers such topics as the effects of exposure to domestic violence, the nature and extent of domestic violence, and the impact of domestic violence on victims and perpetrators.

The need for training is also evident from the fact that many custody evaluators either ignore or minimize domestic violence. Some researchers have documented that custody evaluators may be so preoccupied with promoting visitation and/or joint custody between "friendly parents" that domestic violence easily gets overlooked and parental distrust misinterpreted (Zorza, 1997). One of the important aspects of training is the opportunity for evaluators to hear different perspectives on domestic violence and understand the extensive collaboration that is required within the justice system and across various community services. The extent of this collaboration is apparent from the number of partners that participate in training sessions. An August 2000 training program in Long Beach, California, involved the following agencies (Family Violence & Sexual Assault Institute, 2000):

- Family Violence and Sexual Assault Institute, California
- School of Professional Psychology, Long Beach
- Child Abuse and Domestic Violence Prevention Council, California State University
- Women's Resource Center, Legal Aid Foundation of Long Beach, Statewide California
- Coalition Against Battered Women and New Life Advocacy

The American Bar Association (ABA) has stressed the importance of training lawyers to be more sensitive and effective in responding to clients in domestic violence situations, and has sponsored many seminars and publications about domestic violence. A recent ABA publication on children exposed to domestic violence reads, "Anyone who has committed severe or repetitive abuse to an intimate partner is presumptively not a fit sole or joint custodian for children. Where there is proof of abuse, batterers should be presumed by law to be unfit custodians for their children" (Davidson, 1994).

Domestic violence has been placed on the training agenda for criminal and family court judges in light of the increasing number of cases with domestic violence issues that come before the courts. Training judges is a complex endeavor that requires an understanding of the judicial role and the judiciary's stringent code of ethics. The training needs to be informative, interactive, and cautious, to avoid creating potential biases or violating the principles of an independent judiciary. Judges are the best trainers of other judges, with the assistance of domestic violence consultants and a well-organized curriculum. In the United States and Canada, each state/province is responsible for training judges through state/provincial judges associations, and the federal government is responsible for training federally appointed judges.

Some of the most advanced training for judges has been developed by the National Council of Juvenile and Family Court Judges (NCJFCJ) in partnership with the Family Violence Prevention Fund (FVPF) in San Francisco, California. This training, called "A National Judicial Institute on Domestic Violence: Enhancing Judicial Skill in Domestic Violence Cases" (National Council of Juvenile & Family Court Judges, 2000), is designed to help judges understand victims, perpetrators, and children exposed to domestic violence. Practical courtroom exercises are provided to encourage dialogue about complex cases that pose multiple dilemmas. There is discussion of the role of community services and the challenges in coordinating resources for individual families in crisis. The curriculum covers lethality assessment and safety planning, as well as such issues as a judge's role outside the courtroom. Although there is some variation in state standards on judicial ethics, there is general agreement that judges play a leadership role in ensuring a well-managed courthouse and encouraging access to justice. In addition, there is an increasing focus on cultural issues that address the need to understand individuals and families from different ethnic backgrounds. Overall, these workshops have been well received and have enabled greater networking of judges across the United States (see Lemon, 1990).

Any training of judges has to address the underlying attitudes and beliefs about the nature of domestic violence and its effect on victims and child witnesses. In addressing these issues, educators need to be aware that most judges become extremely frustrated and discouraged at the very idea of facing a child-custody dispute with domestic violence allegations. There is a widely held view that presiding over domestic violence cases is a low priority compared with other judicial appointments that are more likely to garner respect and esteem within the profession (Weissman, 2001). In reality, these cases offer an opportunity to prevent homicides and potentially alter the life course for victims and children. Beyond the safety and quality-of-life issues, successful intervention in these cases also has a profound economic impact that is estimated in the billions for the United States and Canada in terms of victim and perpetrator costs to the health and justice system (Greaves, Hankivsky, & Kingston-Riechers, 1995). Studies have yet to be done to measure the long-term economic impact of children exposed to violence and ending up in the justice, mental health, special education, and health care systems.

Judges play an important role as peers in the recognition of the importance of working with domestic violence cases and ensuring that the community provides the necessary resources to provide access to justice and, hopefully, healing. Although many judges harbor concerns related to the misuse of domestic violence in family court proceedings, in our experience, the more salient issue is the lack of awareness, sensitivity, and appreciation of the relevance of this violence. The efforts of the leading judges in this field are often overwhelmed by the shadows of judges imprisoned by archaic beliefs. For example, a judge reports that one of his colleagues—in considering whether to grant a protective order—asked the victim of domestic violence whether she promised to "honor and obey" her husband. Her affirmative response led the judge to dismiss the application for protection. In similar matters, judges who observe this behavior are encouraged to report it to the appropriate complaints committee rather than shifting the onus to the victim to appeal the case. In other words, the accountability has to rest within the judiciary itself (Newton, 2000).

❖ PROGRAMS AND POLICY DEVELOPMENT

Judges are only as effective as the resources available in their communities. It does not matter how brilliant a judge's decision-making abilities, or how articulate the court judgement, if the programs are not in place to monitor or provide services for domestic violence victims, perpetrators, and their children. Because high-conflict child-custody disputes often have domestic violence as a major factor, these resources are essential. If one were to design an ideal community response, here are some key ingredients for success:

A Well-Designed Courthouse

A courthouse should provide security and comfort to offer families in crisis a safe physical environment for resolving severe conflicts without endangering family members. Separate waiting rooms to ensure safety of domestic violence victims are essential, as well as child-care facilities to protect children from the intimidating courthouse atmosphere.

Representation of Children Involved in Court Proceedings

In most jurisdictions, judges can appoint representation for children in high-conflict child-custody and child-protection disputes. This representation can be in the form of lawyers who are designated as specialists in children's law and possess the ability to access the assistance of social workers (e.g., the Office of the Children's Lawyer in Ontario). This representation also can be operationalized through carefully selected and trained volunteers (e.g., CASA Program in most U.S. states). In either case, proper training in domestic violence is essential. In the absence of such training, the intervention of such services can be detrimental to both the victim of violence and the children.

Access to Legal Aid

Many victims of domestic violence face multiple barriers, including poverty, poor or inadequate housing, and frequent disruptions for their children. Access to legal assistance to manage the various hearings and to gain an advocate is vital to surviving the process. Increasingly, the courts are faced with clients who are representing themselves in child-custody disputes, which places a tremendous burden on the judge to have a safe, effective, and fair hearing on these complex issues. When there is a history of domestic violence, the court has the additional challenge of resolving the power differential between the abused party and the perpetrator. The following are suggestions to potentially mitigate the problems faced by unrepresented parties (Family Violence Prevention Fund, 1995):

- Develop model forms for use in domestic violence child-custody cases that include assessment of risk and protective provisions.
- Provide clerical assistance in completing the forms, particularly for those clients who struggle with language barriers and literacy problems.
- Encourage local law firms or bar associations to do pro bono work.
- Encourage domestic violence advocates to train pro bono lawyers.
- Prioritize legal aid service for domestic violence victims in child-custody proceedings.
- Consider the use of in-camera hearings for abused parties unable to express themselves in open court.
- Offer a list of resources for victims—to promote access to necessary services such as shelters, counseling programs, housing, and emergency financial support.

In our research on abused women separating from batterers, poverty and access to legal advice were critical factors in victims' decision-making abilities (Jaffe, Poisson, Cunningham, & Zerwer, 2001). Some victims choose to live with the certainty of violence, rather than leave to unknown circumstances with potential dangers and disruption for their children. Some victims give up any hope of securing financial support for their children because of the difficulty of navigating the justice system, preferring a batterer who abandons the family over ongoing litigation with uncertain outcomes.

Clearly, many more low-cost or cost-free lawyers and attorneys for battered women in family court and juvenile court are needed, at both the trial and appellate levels. Additionally, victims of domestic violence and their children need significantly speedier access to family law courts. This would require more judges who are prepared to deal with these cases, with enough calendar time to adequately address each case. Family law calendars need to be a much higher priority than they are currently in most jurisdictions. When they continue to be a low priority, with inadequately trained judges and insufficient time, children inevitably suffer.

Well-Trained Custody Evaluators and Mediators

The family court system depends on essential court-related services such as custody evaluations and mediation. Custody evaluators need to have training on domestic violence to understand the impact of domestic violence on children, as well as the relevance of domestic violence to parenting abilities. Because California is the only state in the United States to have legislation that demands this training, many evaluators may not be prepared for domestic violence cases. It is important that lawyers, advocates, and clients themselves screen evaluators for their qualifications and knowledge about domestic violence.

Custody evaluators may play an important role in the ongoing monitoring of child-custody cases following court decisions. Contrary to criminal proceedings wherein the court is kept informed through probation officers about any breaches of conditions, there is no such mechanism within the family court. This lack of monitoring and feedback to the court creates a gap between the evolution of the family and the children's needs and the outdated court decision. This need is exacerbated in domestic violence cases where there may be ongoing issues of stalking, noncompliance with counseling recommendations, visitation and transfer problems, and conflicts over emerging parenting decisions. Rather than offering the court a time-limited snapshot of the family, a custody evaluator could offer a motion picture—more accurately capturing the dynamics and needs of the children. Some authors have pointed out that the role of the batterer as a parent is often inadequately addressed both in the initial assessment and in the evaluation of genuine changes over time (Bancroft & Silverman, 2002).

Mediation services are an essential part of the Family Court process. However, couples with a history of domestic violence do not demonstrate the balance of power and mutual trust and respect necessary for successful mediation. Before families enter mediation there should be individual interviews and domestic violence screening to ensure that inappropriate clients are not placed into mediation (Zorza, 1995). Although some mediators support redesigned mediation services for domestic violence victims and perpetrators to remove face-to-face contact and preserve safety planning, this process is more like shuttle diplomacy/negotiations than traditional mediation and still raises the spectre of victims being coerced into agreement (see Geffner et al., 2000). To illustrate this point, a recent California study found that mediators held joint sessions in nearly half of the couples in which an independent screening interview by a researcher found allegations of domestic violence (Smith, 2002). It was unclear whether the mediators failed to screen for domestic violence, the victims did not voice their allegations to the mediators, or coercion into mediation took place.

In some jurisdictions, mediation is the only affordable and accessible service available to divorcing couples, and abused women may have no other option but to engage in mediation. Although most courts screen out domestic violence cases from mediation, there are many jurisdictions that require mediation, by law or local practice. In such circumstances, the following safeguards should be considered (Family Violence Prevention Fund, 1995):

- Separate sessions with each party on separate days
- A security protocol to ensure the safe arrival and departure of the victim
- A support person to accompany the abused party to mediation
- Provisions in the mediated agreement to ensure ongoing safety for the victim and the children
- Independent review of any agreement by legal counsel before signing
- If mediation fails, provide an alternative dispute resolution process such as a child-custody assessment

Supervised Visitation Centers

Judges may order supervised visits between children and domestic violence perpetrators when there is concern about balancing safety issues with children's interests in maintaining a relationship with a parent. In some communities, there may be formalized visitation centers that can facilitate this contact while monitoring children's progress. In other communities, social workers, professionals in private practice, and volunteers may be supervisors in community facilities or in their own homes. These programs are essential, although not without their own controversies.

Some advocates believe that the programs offer more hope than is realistic; they argue that the idea of supervision should lead to the conclusion of no visitation at all (McMahon & Pence, 1995). However, most judges see supervised visits as an appropriate compromise between competing interests and mechanisms to ensure safety (Sheeran & Hampton, 1999).

Courts can promote the safety of abused women and their children by specifying certain conditions as part of the court order such as the following (National Council of Juvenile and Family Court Judges, 1994):

- Not requiring or encouraging contact between the parties
- Ordering visitation in a location physically separate from the abused party
- Requiring transfer of the children between the parents in the presence of a neutral third party and in a protected setting
- Starting with short, daytime visits in a public place and increasing the length of the visits only if things are going well
- Including a provision for no alcohol or drug consumption by the visiting parent, as well as providing direction as to the immediate consequences of violation of the provision
- Placing limits on overnight visitation
- Requiring the perpetrator to successfully complete a batterer's intervention program, drug/alcohol program, or a parenting-education program before being permitted visitation
- Building in automatic return dates for court to monitor how the order is working out
- Not ordering the victim into counseling with the perpetrator as a precondition of custody or visitation

To truly become safe places for children and adult victims, supervised visitation centers require staff trained in working with perpetrators and victims of domestic violence, and sliding fee scales subsidized by the state or federal government to ensure that the service is accessible and affordable. Increasingly, supervised visitation centers are developing standards of practice so that that there is greater consistency and quality in the delivery of supervised access (Supervised Access Program Ministry of the Attorney General, 2000).

Support Programs for Victims of Domestic Violence

Anyone who has experienced domestic violence and must deal with a custody or visitation dispute requires considerable support. Although "justice for all" is a goal of the court system, abuse victims are disadvantaged without access to well-trained and experienced lawyers who specialize in family law. In addition to legal support, abuse victims need emotional support, counselling to cope with the abuse trauma, and practical advice to navigate the complex and time-consuming court hearings. For highly contested custody cases with allegations of domestic violence, abused women report many years of drained financial and emotional resources (Sinclair, 2000).

Many of the developments in services for abused women have come as a result of the criminal justice prosecution of domestic violence cases. Victim crisis services offered by local police departments and victim support services attached to prosecutors' offices have become commonplace. However, except for the extension of the role of domestic violence advocates helping women negotiate both criminal and family (civil) legal systems, these services have not developed on the family law side of the justice system.

Across North America, there is great variation in the nature, affordability, and access to services in child-custody proceedings. In some communities, shelters for abused women have identified this issue as a priority and have organized support groups and client-education programs to prepare women for custody proceedings (Sinclair, 2000). In other communities, a fortunate woman may find lawyers and domestic violence experts who do work on a pro bono basis. Usually, there is information available from local women's shelters or statewide coalitions about qualified legal and mental health professionals with knowledge of, and sensitivity to, these issues.

Meaningful programs are also needed to assist battered women who are targeted by the juvenile court system, so that they can successfully protect their children from witnessing further abuse, rather than having their children removed due to "failure to protect" them. For this reason, one publicly funded service that may not be appropriate in domestic violence cases is the child-protection agency. Certainly there are extreme cases where children are exposed to violence and neither parent is capable of protecting the children from further harm, no matter how many resources are offered to individual family members. However, there is a growing concern among domestic violence advocates that abused women may be revictimized by poorly trained and inadequately funded child-protection services (Weithorn, 2001).

In many jurisdictions, there is evidence that abused women are held accountable for not protecting their children from domestic violence, whereas the perpetrator of the violence bears no responsibility (Schechter & Edleson, 1999). Some states have made exposure to violence grounds for mandatory reporting of child abuse, without the proper training and resources. After this requirement was introduced in Minnesota and Florida, the reported cases of child abuse increased so dramatically that the child-protection system became overwhelmed and was unable to respond in any meaningful manner (Weithorn, 2001). In Canada, concerns have been raised about the routine filing of police domestic violence reports with child-protection services, without proper assessments of needs and risk (Joint Committee on Domestic Violence, 1999). The recent trend in both the United States and Canada is to enhance collaboration between domestic violence advocates and child-protection workers to improve services, coordinate programs, and prevent revictimization of the abused (Schechter & Edleson, 1999).

In cases of prolonged litigation, support for abused women in child-custody proceedings may require years of ongoing services. Some batterers will use the family court as an arena to extend the same struggle for power, control, and dominance as took place in the marriage. Every court hearing leads to another hearing, irrespective of the outcome. In many cases, the batterer's continued efforts to pursue custody or extend visitation rights are renewed attempts to annoy, harass, and threaten the ex-partner. In these circumstances, there may be a need for a support group with other survivors of domestic violence who have experience in these matters (Sinclair, 2000). There may also be a need for the court to stop the batterer from continuing to use the court system to harass the victim.

Programs for Batterers

An essential step in holding batterers responsible for their violence is enrollment in a batterers' intervention program. If there are parallel criminal proceedings and a conviction, most judges will consider a probation order with a condition to attend such a program (Healy et al.,

1998). These programs should meet basic standards set by the state or relevant government department. Programs may vary in length from 26 weeks to 52 weeks and include an advocate who maintains contact with the victims to ensure their safety and the cessation of violence (Healy et al., 1998).

Programs for batterers have shown some modest success, especially in the context of an overall, coordinated community response and zero tolerance for domestic violence (see Dutton, 1995; Healy et al., 1998). The most significant problem is getting past batterers' denials and finding the appropriate intervention. Many batterers refuse to acknowledge their role in the violence. They may make limited efforts to receive assistance at a point of crisis, for example, when their partner threatens to leave unless they get help, but rarely follow through. Most of those who contact batterers' intervention programs to request information never make it past the intake interview, let alone complete the program (Healy et al., 1998).

Another significant problem is referral to inappropriate programs. Some batterers may attend an anger-management group that does not recognize the fact that the batterer is rarely angry or violent in situations outside the home. Batterers may convince their partner to attend-couples counseling, which is contraindicated for safety reasons as well as concerns that the victim will be blamed for the violence. Batterers may attribute their violence to alcohol or drug abuse. Although alcohol and drug abuse can be associated with domestic violence and can increase the level of risk of dangerous or lethal violence, it is not the cause of violence. Batterers with substance abuse problems require two separate program interventions. All too often, however, lawyers convince judges that their clients' violence is being remedied by attendance at AA meetings or visits with a family doctor (Healy et al., 1998).

Batterers are not a homogeneous group, and some require more intensive assessment and treatment programs. The standardized batterers' intervention program is ideal for individuals who show a pattern of physical and emotional abuse in their homes but not in the community. Batterers who are generally violent and antisocial in their values, attitudes, and behaviors may be beyond any known treatment in the community. The only issues to address are safety, institutional management, and community supervision. A small number of batterers may have significant mental health problems that require medication and intensive therapy as an adjunct to other interventions. The research on batterer typology and batterer intervention is still in its infancy. Many questions have been raised about the effectiveness of treatment programs, especially for various ethnic groups. For example, some practitioners believe that individuals of Asian descent do not respond well to elements of group programs that promote confrontation and shame about abusive behavior (Healy et al., 1998).

As the research continues to develop in this area, practice will be bound by essential principles in responding to batterers, which include accountability and responsibility for violent behavior, acknowledgment of the impact of violence on victims and children, commitment to change, monitoring of change, and safety planning for victims. This area also requires coordination in the justice system to ensure that changes in supervision of visits or increasing contact with children is predicated on successful attendance, participation, and change in a batterers' program. This coordination is essential to ensure the safety of abused women and their children. Recent studies in major cities suggest that batterers' intervention programs can reduce new incidents of violence in approximately half of the cases over a 15-month follow-up period (Gondolf & Jones, 2001). The critical issues appear to be the extent that the court mandates the intervention and finds effective means to monitor compliance with these orders (Gondolf, 2002).

Programs for Children Exposed to Domestic Violence

Children from high-conflict divorces, especially when there is a history of domestic violence, require ongoing support and counseling as well as freedom from prolonged litigation (see Johnston, 1994). As discussed in Chapter 2, children may be exposed to a range of violence; a host of risk and protective factors determine the degree of adjustment problems they experience.

Some children are highly traumatized by the violence and require intensive, individual counseling to deal with the aftermath of the parental separation. In some cases, the violence appears never-ending, as continuing domestic violence occurs during visitation exchanges (Zorza, 1995). For these children, there is no healing until there is safety and an end to the violence. Individual counseling will be required to address their trauma symptoms and the impact of the trauma on their daily functioning in school and community activities. Obviously, the intervention must be appropriate to the child's age and stage of development. For younger children, the intervention must focus on the emotional and physical health of the mother as principal caretaker, because this relationship is the foundation for the child's attachment and recovery from the trauma. To assist mental health professionals, several authors have addressed the special needs of children exposed to domestic violence (Arroyo & Eth, 1995; McAlister-Groves, 1999; Silvern, Karyl, & Landis, 1995).

Across the United States and Canada, there are a number of group programs for child witnesses of domestic violence, irrespective of their level of adjustment problems (see McAlister-Groves, 1999; Peled & Edleson, 1995). These programs are mainly targeted to children 8 to 12 years of age, and focus on preventing long-term destructive attitudes and behaviors that give rise to violence within intimate relationships (Peled & Edleson, 1995). These groups help children understand that there are alternatives to violence in resolving conflicts. They are encouraged not to take responsibility for violence in their family, and to develop a safety plan to utilize in the event that domestic violence occurs (Peled & Edleson, 1995). The programs have been implemented in a number of settings—including women's shelters, schools, mental health centers, and child-protection facilities—in partnership with domestic violence advocates (Jaffe et al., 1996). Many of the concepts have been extended to adolescents in specialized groups to address both dating violence and the broader roots of violence in society (see Wolfe & Jaffe, 1999).

Large numbers of children show no immediate symptoms related to exposure to violence, and there is some debate as to whether all children living with domestic violence should be part of an intervention program. Participation in a recognized program can offer some benefits as a secondary prevention strategy, because long-term effects of exposure to violence may only become apparent in the adolescent and early adult years in the context of dating and intimate relationships (Wolfe & Jaffe, 1999). However, although intervention programs may have some prophylactic effects, this issue has not been researched thus far. Most outcome studies only examine the short-term benefits of groups (Peled & Edleson, 1995).

Coordination of Services

A community response to domestic violence is only as strong as its weakest link. Domestic violence requires thoughtful and sensitive responses from different service agencies in different systems, including the courts. Abused women who try to leave batterers face overwhelming odds in finding safety and meaningful access to justice and support systems. Consider the following hypothetical case:

> Mary Jones leaves Bob Jones after 15 years of marriage and two children, Tom and Jennifer, ages 12 and 10. The last 10 years of the marriage were filled with physical, sexual, and emotional abuse in which Bob dominated and humiliated Mary on a regular basis. There is no documentation of the violence except for Mary's discussions with her family doctor and conversations with her sister living in a distant city. Because of the recent escalation of the violence, Mary fears for her life and has brought the children to a shelter. The police are called to report the detailed threats on Mary's life and the most recent assault. Mary contacts a family lawyer to apply for a restraining order, possession of the matrimonial house, and interim custody of the children with supervised visitation by Bob on Saturday afternoons for 3 hours, on the condition that he enroll in a batterers' program. Bob denies the history of violence and claims that Mary is exaggerating conflicts in the marriage to further her claim for custody, support, and possession of the house. In fact, he alleges that Mary has been turning the children against him. He feels that the children are in danger of becoming alienated from him, should the court support her requests.

This case demonstrates the complexity of the issues facing the community in assisting families like the Joneses. The police will have to conduct an initial assessment of the allegations, decide on charges, and complete a risk assessment (see the "Dangerous Suspect Assessment" form developed by the Duluth Police Department, Duluth Police Department, 1997). The family court will have to coordinate its proceedings with the criminal court. Bob will be presumed innocent of the allegations in the criminal court but the family court judge will be asked to make a finding of domestic violence, on the preponderence of the evidence, in order to decide custody and visitation arrangements. A custody evaluation will be needed as well as appropriate counseling programs for each family member. This case presents a challenge for the training and policies of the police as well as many other community partners, and illustrates the need to coordinate various services at different stages of the justice system in both criminal and family proceedings. The outcome of this case could take years of hearings and interventions. Discouraged by the delays and complexities of the proceedings, Mary could decide to return to Bob because he offers more resources than the piecemeal and inconsistent community responses. As with many abused women, she may decide to return to Bob because she is fearful of losing her children in a child-custody dispute. Obviously, this scenario is even more complex when additional barriers to service, such as poverty or differences in language and culture, are present.

Over the past 10 years, there has been increasing recognition that an effective community response to domestic violence depends on an integrated community approach in which the various professionals and systems act in unison through standardized protocols, policies, standards, and training. A starting point toward achieving this goal is a local council or coordinating committee on domestic violence, bringing together the various players and agencies. The council can be created within the community around the court system to ensure collaboration on behalf of victims, perpetrators, and children.

One well-established model council has roots in Santa Clara County, California (San Jose) and has benefited from judicial leadership (Edwards, 1992). The usual goals of such a council are coordination of services, promotion of prevention effort, improvement of initial response to domestic violence, research, training, and the development of strategies for legislative reform. Membership usually includes defense counsels (public defenders), prosecutors, probation officers, judges, police, batterers' intervention program staff, women's advocates, social services, health care professionals, children's services, and the faith community. In Santa Clara County there are also a number of council subcommittees that coordinate various projects on public education, research, court system policies, and legislation review. One of the first Canadian coordinating committees on domestic violence was established in London, Ontario, in 1980 as a response to research on the effectiveness of police interventions with abused women (Jaffe et al., 1996). The committee helped develop innovative programs for victims of domestic violence, batterers, and children growing up in violent homes. The committee now has over 25 members and is responsible for coordinating and consulting on dozens of projects including a recent study on the impact of poverty and violence on women and children's adjustment and access to services after separation (The London Coordinating Committee to End Woman Abuse, 2001).

Although most coordinating committees have tended to focus on the criminal prosecution of domestic violence and the development of support services, the link between domestic violence and child custody is now beginning to receive the attention it deserves.

❖ CONCLUSION

Responding to domestic violence in a sensitive and effective manner is a challenge for any community. Often decisions are made that may have life-or-death consequences. When domestic violence occurs in the context of a child-custody dispute, the dilemmas multiply. This concept is summarized by the comments of Barbara Hart (1998) in describing the need of the justice system to provide safety and accountability in domestic violence cases:

> Safety is not simple. Minimally, it entails being free of violence and coercion. But safety goes well beyond and includes the ability to negotiate life's daily challenges without having decisions intruded upon and contravened by a controlling partner. It includes the confidence that the battering parent will not dispute the routines of children. It is the freedom from public and private denigration from an abusive spouse. It is a cessation of stalking. It is the knowledge that disagreement with the child's father will not precipitate violent retaliation. (p. 3)

This chapter has outlined the range of services, training, legislation, and community collaboration that is demanded in these circumstances. Twenty-five years ago, domestic violence was a hidden crime and the women's movement and the development of shelters were the only signs of recognition. Now, every professional in every sector (health, social service, mental health, education, and law) has an obligation to understand the nature and scope of this problem. Without effective services, policies, training, and legislation, abused women and children will become painful statistics.

Every community must survey the resources available to respond to domestic violence. Some jurisdictions have proposed a report card to measure progress on services for victims, perpetrators, and children as part of an integrated approach to the problem (Joint Committee on Domestic Violence, 1999). Across the United States and Canada there is an uneven distribution of training, collaboration, and resources depending on local champions for domestic violence awareness and prioritization of funding needs (Jaffe et al., 1996). Access to services should be universal and training for all professionals should be consistent.

Child-custody disputes in which domestic violence is a factor demand the highest level of coordination within the justice system, and between the justice system and human services. Courts are expected to make difficult decisions that require the expertise of custody evaluators, and resources such as supervised visitation centers, to implement. A brilliant, sensitive judge is totally impotent in making meaningful decisions without the ability to carry out and monitor critical interventions.

To add complexity to the court process, there is rarely a final decision. The nature of child development means that frequent adjustments to custody and visitation planning are necessary. For example, supervised visitation is a time-limited remedy, which involves ongoing evaluation of the batterer's progress in treatment, risk assessments, the wishes and interests of the children, and the mother's ability to maintain her safety plan. To juggle competing interests, the court depends on up-to-date, accurate information from all the parties. Time and resources are essential to manage such a system (Jaffe & Geffner, 1998).

We have written this book to help parents and caring legal and mental health professionals better understand the link between domestic violence and child-custody disputes. Traditionally, this link has been ignored. As long as parents did not directly abuse their children, little consideration was given to the impact of spousal violence on child adjustment. In our view, batterers, by the very nature of their behavior, cannot be good parents. Modeling violence as a means of resolving conflict and illustrating ways of controlling and humiliating another parent are not acceptable. When parents socialize their children into violence and sexism, the whole community suffers in the long run.

The divorce literature has ignored domestic violence for far too long. Minimizing domestic violence by calling it "conflict" or "poor communication" is a disservice to victims, perpetrators, and children exposed to the violence. We hope that this book provokes and stimulates other resources and practitioners to find more effective strategies to help family members in these circumstances and prevent the terrible toll that domestic violence has taken on many divorcing couples and their children.

Appendix

Abuse Observation Checklist (ABOC)

Please indicate how often the following behaviors were done to you by your partner, were done by you to your partner, and which, if any, of these incidences were witnessed by your child(ren). Responses should refer to the duration of the relationship (e.g., not just years of marriage).

Name:________________________________ Date:____________________

Clinician:________________________________

Children's Names: Child A: ____________________ Age:______ Sex:______

Child B: ____________________ Age:______ Sex:______

Child C: ____________________ Age:______ Sex:______

Child D: ____________________ Age:______ Sex:______

	You did to your partner				Your partner did to you				How long since last occurrence?				Occurred before/after separation?		Which child(ren) witnessed?	Last time child(ren) witnessed?		
	0	1-3	3-10	>10	0	1-3	3-10	>10	0-6m	6-12m	1-2y	+2y	Before	After	A,B,C and/or D	<1y	1-2y	>2y
PHYSICAL ABUSE																		
Threw something at you/him/her																		
Pushed, grabbed, shoved, or wrestled you/him/her																		
Scratched, slapped, pinched you/him/her or pulled your/his/her hair																		
Kicked, hit, punched, or beat you/him/her																		
Threatened you/him/her with a knife or gun																		
Used a knife or gun																		
Attempted to smother, strangle, or hang you/him/her with an object																		
Put dangerous substance (e.g., gasoline, acid) on your/his/her body																		
Burned your/his/her body																		
Physically restrained you/him/her by holding or by tying you/him/her up																		

	You did to your partner				Your partner did to you				How long since last occurrence?				Occurred before/after separation?		Which child(ren) witnessed?	Last time child(ren) witnessed?		
	0	1-3	3-10	>10	0	1-3	3-10	>10	0-6m	6-12m	1-2y	+2y	Before	After	A,B,C and/or D	<1y	1-2y	>2y
Dragged or pulled you/him/her																		
Used force or threat of force to get you/him/her to eat/drink something (including alcohol or drugs) or restricted you/him/her from these activities																		
Used force or threat of force to restrict you/him/her from using toilet, shower, bath or otherwise attending to hygiene																		
Restricted you/him/her from taking prescribed medication or obtaining needed medical treatment																		
Threw hot liquid on you/him/her																		
Used car to attempt to run over you/him/her																		
Put excrement on your/his/her body																		
INJURY																		
Lost hair																		
Cuts																		
Burns																		
Bruises																		
Black eye(s)																		
Sprains/strains																		
Lost teeth																		
Human bite																		
Broken eardrum																		

	You did to your partner				Your partner did to you				How long since last occurrence?				Occurred before/after separation?		Which child(ren) witnessed?	Last time child(ren) witnessed?		
	0	1-3	3-10	>10	0	1-3	3-10	>10	0-6m	6-12m	1-2y	+2y	Before	After	A,B,C and/or D	<1y	1-2y	>2y
Joint or spinal cord injury																		
Broken nose or jaw																		
Other broken bones, including ribs																		
Concussion																		
Internal injury																		
Permanent injury (blindness, loss of hearing, disfigurement, chronic pain)																		
You/He/She required medical treatment, but received none																		
You/He/She required medical treatment/outpatient or EMR																		
You/He/She required hospitalization																		

SEXUAL ABUSE
Type of unwanted sexual behavior:

Vaginal or anal intercourse																		
Fellatio or cunnilingus																		
Sexual behavior with another adult (not partner) or with a child																		
Watched nudity or sexual behavior involving another																		
Viewed pornography film, photographs																		
Filmed you/him/her while engaged in sexual activity																		
Forced nudity or made to dress in sexually provocative clothing																		

	You did to your partner				Your partner did to you				How long since last occurrence?				Occurred before/after separation?		Which child(ren) witnessed?	Last time child(ren) witnessed?		
	0	1-3	3-10	>10	0	1-3	3-10	>10	0-6m	6-12m	1-2y	+2y	Before	After	A,B,C and/or D	<1y	1-2y	>2y
Unwanted objects were inserted into your/his/her vagina/rectum																		
Required to be involved with an animal in a sexual way																		
PSYCHOLOGICAL ABUSE																		
Coercion and Threats:																		
Made or carried out threats to do something to hurt you/him/her or someone else																		
Threatened to kill you/him/her or someone else																		
Threatened to leave relationship																		
He/She threatened to commit suicide																		
Threatened to report you/him/her to welfare, social services, police																		
Attempted to get you/him/her to drop charges against the abuser																		
Attempted to get you/him/her to engage in illegal activities																		
Intimidation:																		
Instilled fear in you/him/her by looks, gestures, actions																		
Smashed objects or destroyed your/his/her property																		
Abused your/his/her family pets																		
Displayed weapons																		

	You did to your partner				Your partner did to you				How long since last occurrence?				Occurred before/after separation?		Which child(ren) witnessed?	Last time child(ren) witnessed?		
	0	1-3	3-10	>10	0	1-3	3-10	>10	0-6m	6-12m	1-2y	+2y	Before	After	A,B,C and/or D	<1y	1-2y	>2y
Emotional Abuse:																		
Insulted, called you/him/her names or used "put downs"																		
Attempted to make you/him/her feel crazy																		
Humiliated you/him/her with words or gestures																		
Attempted to make you/him/her feel guilty																		
Verbally raged at you/him/her																		
Engaged in extramarital affairs																		
Withheld sex from you/him/her																		
Attempted to control what you/he/she did																		
Attempted to control what you/he/she read/watched on TV or listened to																		
Isolation:																		
Attempted to limit your/his/her involvement with others																		
Used jealousy to justify actions against you/him/her																		
Restricted your/his/her use of the phone																		
Restricted your/his/her leaving the house																		
Minimization, Denial, and Blaming:																		
Minimized or denied abuse and not take your/his/her concerns about it seriously																		

	You did to your partner				Your partner did to you				How long since last occurrence?				Occurred before/after separation?		Which child(ren) witnessed?	Last time child(ren) witnessed?		
	0	**1-3**	**3-10**	**>10**	**0**	**1-3**	**3-10**	**>10**	**0-6m**	**6-12m**	**1-2y**	**+2y**	**Before**	**After**	**A,B,C and/or D**	**<1y**	**1-2y**	**>2y**
Blamed you/him/her for the abuse or shifted responsibility for the abusive behavior onto someone else																		
Use of Children to Control You:																		
Attempted to make you/him/her feel guilty about children																		
Used children to relay messages to you/him/her																		
Used visitation to harass you/him/her																		
Threatened to take children away (e.g., custody, kidnapping) from you/him/her																		
Threatened to abuse children																		
ECONOMIC/RESOURCE ABUSE																		
Attempted to prevent you/him/her from getting/keeping a job or going to school																		
Required you/him/her to ask for money																		
Controlled the money by either giving you an allowance or controlled your use of money																		
Made major decisions without your/his/her equal participation																		
Withheld information about/access to family resources																		

References

Achenbach, T. M., & Edelbrock, C. (1983). *Manual for the child behavior checklist and revised child behavior profile.* Burlington: University of Vermont Department of Psychiatry.

Ackerman, M. J. (1995). *Clinician's guide to child custody evaluations.* New York: John Wiley.

Aiken, J., & Murphy, J. (2000). Evidence issues in domestic violence civil cases. *Family Law Quarterly, 34,* 43–62.

Alberta Law Reform Institute. (1995). Domestic abuse: Toward an effective legal response. *Report for Discussion, 15.*

Amato, P. R., Loomis, L. S., & Booth, A. (1995). Parental divorce, marital conflict, and offspring well-being during early adulthood. *Social Forces, 73,* 895–915.

American Bar Association. (1994). *The impact of domestic violence on children.*

American Medical Association. (1992). Violence against women. *Journal of the American Medical Association, 267,* 107–112.

American Psychiatric Association. (2000). *Diagnostic and statistical manual of mental disorders (DSM-IV-TR).* Washington, DC: Author.

American Psychological Association. (1994). Guidelines for child custody evaluations in divorce proceedings. *American Psychologist, 49,* 677–680.

American Psychological Association. (1996). *Violence and the family.* Washington, DC: Author.

Arroyo, W., & Eth, S. (1995). Assessment following violence-witnessing trauma. In E. Peled, P. G. Jaffe, & J. L. Edleson (Eds.), *Ending the cycle of violence: Community Reponses to children of battered women* (pp. 27–42). Thousand Oaks, CA: Sage.

Astor, H. (1994). Swimming against the tide: Keeping violent men out of mediation. In J. Stubbs (Ed.), *Women, male violence, and the law* (pp. 147-173). Sydney, Australia: Institute of Criminology, Sydney University Law School.

Bala, N. (1999). A report from Canada's "gender war zone": Reforming the child-related provisions of the *Divorce Act. Canadian Journal of Family Law, 16,* 163–227.

Bala, N. (2000). A differential legal approach to the effects of spousal abuse on children: A Canadian context. In R.Geffner, P. G. Jaffe, & M. Suderman (Eds.), *Children exposed to domestic violence: Current issues in research, intervention, prevention, and policy development* (pp. 301–328). Binghamton, NY: Haworth Press.

Bala, N. (2001). *Spousal abuse and children: Issues in family law proceedings.* Paper presented at Family Law Judicial Education Program of the National Judicial Institute. Halifax, Nova Scotia. http://qsilver.queensu.ca/law/papers/spouseabuse&kids.htm

Bala, N. (2001, June). *Spousal abuse and children: Issues in Canadian family law proceedings.* Paper presented at the International Conference on Children Exposed to Domestic Violence, London, ON.

Bala, N., Bertrand, L., Paetsch, J., Knoppers, B., Hornick, J., Noel, J. F., Boudreau, L., & Miklas, S. (1998). *Spousal violence in custody and access disputes: Recommendations for reform.* Ottawa, ON: Status of Women Canada.

Bancroft, L., & Silverman, J. (2002). *The batterer as a parent: Addressing the impact of domestic violence on family dynamics.* Thousand Oaks, CA: Sage.

Behrens, J. (1996). Ending the silence, but . . . family violence under the Family Law Reform Act 1995. *Australian Journal of Family Law, 10,* 35–47.

Bowermaster, J. M. (1998). Relocation custody disputes involving domestic violence. *University of Kansas Law Review, 46*(3), 433–463.

Bowermaster, J., & Johnson, D. (1998, October). *The role of domestic violence in family court child custody determinations: An interdisciplinary investigation.* Paper presented at the Fourth International Conference on Children Exposed to Domestic Violence, San Diego, CA.

Braver, S. L., & O'Connell, D. (1998). *Divorced dads: Shattering the myths.* New York: Penguin Putnam.

Briere, J. (1997a). *Psychological assessment of adult posttraumatic states.* Washington, DC: American Psychological Association.

Briere, J. (1997b). *Trauma symptom checklist for children: Professional manual.* Odessa, FL: Psychological Assessment Resources.

Bureau of Justice Statistics. (2001). *Homicide trends in the U.S.: Intimate homicide.* Washington, DC: U.S. Department of Justice.

Busch, R. (1994). "Don't throw bouquets at me (judges) will say we're in love": An analysis of New Zealand judges' attitudes towards domestic violence. In J. Stubbs (Ed.), *Women, male violence, and the law, Institute of criminology monograph series* (pp. 104–146). The Institute of Criminology Monograph Series No. 6. Sydney, Australia: Federation Press.

Busch, R., & Robertson, N. (2000). Innovative approaches to child custody and domestic violence in New Zealand: The effects of law reform on the discourses of battering. In R.A.Geffner, P. G. Jaffe, & M. Suderman (Eds.), *Children exposed to domestic violence: Current issues in research, intervention, prevention and policy development* (pp. 269–300). Binghamton, NY: Haworth Press.

Campbell, J. C. (1995). *Assessing dangerousness: Violence by sexual offenders, batterers, and child abusers.* Thousand Oaks, CA: Sage.

Campbell, J. C., Sharps, P., & Glass, N. (2001). Risk assessment for intimate partner homicide. In G. F. Pinard & L. Pagani (Eds.), *Clinical assessment of dangerousness: Empirical contributions* (pp. 136–157). New York: Cambridge University Press.

Canadian Centre for Justice Statistics. (2000). *Family violence in Canada: A statistical profile.* Ottawa, ON, Canada: Statistics Canada.

Chisholm, B. A., & MacNaughton, H. C. (1990). *Custody/access assessments: A practical guide for lawyers and assessors*. Toronto, ON, Canada: Carswell.

Cook, P. W. (1997). *Abused men: The hidden side of domestic violence*. Westport, CT: Praeger Publishers/Greenwood Publishing Group.

Cruz, J. M., & Firestone, J. M. (1998). Exploring violence and abuse in gay male relationships. *Violence and Victims, 13,* 159–173.

Cummings, E. M., & Davies, P. T. (1994). *Children and marital conflict.* New York: Guilford.

Cummings, E. M., Iannotti, R. J., & Zahn-Waxler, C. (1985). Influence of conflict between adults on the emotions and aggression of young children. *Developmental Psychology, 21,* 495–507.

Dallam, S. (1999). The parental alientation syndrome: Is it scientific? In E. T. St. Charles & L. Crook (Eds.), *Expose: The failure of family courts to protect children from abuse in custody disputes* (pp. 67–93). Los Gatos, CA: Our Children Our Future Charitable Foundation.

Dalton, C. (1999). When paradigms collide: Protecting battered parents and their children in the family court system. *Family and Conciliation Courts Review, 37,* 273–296.

Davidson, H. A. (1994). *The impact of domestic violence on children: A report to the president of the American Bar Association* (2nd rev. ed.). Chicago, IL: American Bar Association.

Davidson, H. A. (1995). Child abuse and domestic violence: Legal connections and controversies. *Family Law Quarterly, 29,* 357–373.

Davis, P. (1989, May 10). Jury finds Friedlander guilty in wife's death. *Washington Post,* p. D5.

De Becker, G. (1997). *The gift of fear: Survival signals that protect us from violence.* Boston: Little Brown.

Department of the Attorney General. (1984). *Attorney General's Task Force on Family Violence.* Washington, DC: Author.

Dewar, J., & Parker, S. (1999). The impact of the new Part VII Family Law Act 1975. *Australian Journal of Family Law, 13,* 96–116.

Dobash, R. E., & Dobash, R. P. (1992). *Women, violence and social change.* London, England: Routledge.

Dobash, R. E., Dobash, R. P., Cavanagh, K., & Lewis, R. (2000). *Changing violent men.* Thousand Oaks, CA: Sage.

Dobash, R. P., Dobash, R. E., Wilson, M., & Daly, M. (1992). The myth of sexual symmetry in marital violence. *Social Problems, 39,* 71–91.

Duluth Police Department. (1997). *Dangerous suspect assessment.* Duluth, MN: Duluth City Attorney's Office.

Dutton, D. G. (1995). *The batterer: A psychological profile*. New York: Basic Books.

Dutton, M. A. (1992). *Empowering and healing the battered woman: A model for assessment and intervention*. New York: Springer.

Dutton, M. A. (1996). Battered women's strategic response to violence: The role of context. In J. L. Edleson & Z. C. Eisikovits (Eds.), *Future interventions with battered women and their families* (pp. 105–124). Thousand Oaks, CA: Sage.

Dutton, M. A., & Goodman, L. A. (1994). Posttraumatic stress disorder among battered women: Analysis of legal implications. *Behavioral Sciences and the Law, 12,* 215–234.

Echlin, C., & Osthoff, B. (2000). Child protection workers and battered women's advocates working together to end violence against women and children. In R. Geffner, P. G. Jaffe, & M. Suderman (Eds.), *Children exposed to domestic violence* (pp. 207–219). New York: Haworth.

Edleson, J. L. (1999). The overlap between child maltreatment and woman battering. *Violence Against Women, 5,* 134–154.

Edwards, L. P. (1992). Reducing family violence: The role of the family violence council. *Juvenile and Family Court Journal, 43,* 1–18.

Elrod, L. D., & Spector, R.G. (2001). A review of the year in family law: Redefining families, reforming custody jurisdiction and refining support laws. *Family Law Quarterly, 34,* 607–620.

Emery, R. E. (1982). Interparental conflict and the children of discord and divorce. *Psychological Bulletin, 92,* 310–330.

Faller, K. C. (1998). "The parental alienation syndrome: What is it and what data support it?": Reply. *Child Maltreatment: Journal of the American Professional Society on the Abuse of Children, 3,* 312–313. Family Violence & Sexual Assault Institute. (2000). *Practical applications for custody evaluation: Domestic violence training*. San Diego, CA: Author.

Frederick, L. (2001). *Effective interventions in domestic violence cases: Context is everything.* Minneapolis, MN: Battered Women's Justice Project.

Gardner, R. A. (1992). *The parental alienation syndrome: A guide for mental health and legal professionals.* Cresskill, NJ: Creative Therapeutics.

Garrity, C. B., & Baris, M. A. (1994). *Caught in the middle: Protecting the children of high-conflict divorce.* San Francisco: Jossey-Bass.

Geffner, R. A., Jaffe, P. G., & Sudermann, M. (2000). *Children exposed to domestic violence: Current issues in research, intervention, prevention and policy development*. Binghamton, NY: Haworth Press.

Gondolf, E. W. (2002). *Batterer intervention systems: Issues, outcomes, and recommendations.* Thousand Oaks, CA: Sage.

Gondolf, E. W., & Jones, A. S. (2001). The program effect of batterers programs in three cities. *Violence and Victims, 6,* 693–704.

Graham-Bermann, S. A. (1996). Family worries: Assessment of interpersonal anxiety in children from violence and nonviolent families. *Journal of Clinical Child Psychology, 25,* 280–287.

Graham-Bermann, S. A., & Edleson, J. L. (2001). *Domestic violence in the lives of children: The future of research, intervention, and social policy.* Washington, DC: American Psychological Association.

Graham-Bermann, S. A., & Levendosky, A. A. (1998). Traumatic stress symptoms in children of battered women. *Journal of Interpersonal Violence, 13,* 111–128.

Graycar, R. (1995). The relevance of violence in family law decision making. *Australian Journal of Family Law, 9*(1), 58–69.

Greaves, L., Hankivsky, O., & Kingston-Riechers, J. (1995). *Selected estimates of the cost of violence against women.* London, ON: Centre for Research on Violence Against Women and Children.

Grych, J. H., Seid, M., & Fincham, F. D. (1992). Assessing marital conflict from the child's perspective: The Children's Perception of Interparental Conflict Scale. *Child Development, 63,* 558–572.

Hart, B. J. (1990). Assessing whether batterers will kill. In Pennsylvania Coalition Against Domestic Violence (Eds.), *Confronting domestic violence: Effective police response.* Harrisburg, PA: PCADV.

Hart, B. J. (1992). State codes on domestic violence: Analysis, commentary and recommendations. *Juvenile and Family Court Journal, 43,* 1–81.

Hart, B. J. (1998). *Safety and accountability: The underpinnings of a just justice system.* Harrisburg, PA: Pennsylvania Coalition Against Domestic Violence.

Hartman, A. (1996). Social policy as a context for lesbian and gay families: The political is personal. In J. Laird & R.-J. Green (Eds.), *Lesbians and gays in couples and families: A handbook for therapists* (pp. 69–85). San Francisco: Jossey-Bass.

Hassler, R., Johnson, B., Town, M., & Websdale, N. (2001). Lethality assessments as integral parts of providing full faith and credit guarantees. Violence against women online resources [Online]. Available: http://www.vaw.umn.edu/FFC/chapter9.html

Healy, K., Smith, C., & O'Sullivan, C. (1998). *Batterer intervention: Program approaches and criminal justice strategies.* Washington, DC: National Institute of Justice, U.S. Department of Justice.

Henning, K., Leitenberg, H., Coffey, P., Turner, T., & Bennett, R. T. (1996). Long-term psychological and social impact of witnessing physical conflict between parents. *Journal of Interpersonal Violence, 11,* 35–51.

Herman, J. L. (1992). *Trauma and recovery.* New York: Basic Books.

Hetherington, E. M., & Kelly, J. (2002). *For better or for worse: Divorce reconsidered.* New York: Norton.

Hirst, A. (2002, March). *Child custody mediation and domestic violence.* Paper presented at the 2002 Family Court Services Statewide Educational Institute, Long Beach, CA.

Hoff, P. M. (1998). The ABC's of the UCCJEA: Interstate child-custody practice under the new act and Uniform Child-Custody Jurisdiction and Enforcement Act. *Family Law Quarterly, 32,* 267–299.

Holden, G. W., Geffner, R., & Jouriles, E. N. E. (1998). *Children exposed to marital violence: Theory, research, and applied issues.* Washington, DC: American Psychological Association.

H.R. Con. Res. 172, Rep. Constance Morella, Vol. 136 Cong. Rec., page S 18252-04 (Oct. 25, 1990).

Irving, H. H., & Benjamin, M. (1996). Mobility rights and children's interests: Empirically-based first principles as a guide to effective parenting plans. *Canadian Family Law Quarterly, 13,* 249–260.

Jaffe, P. G. (1995). Children of domestic violence: Special challenges in custody and visitation dispute resolution. In N. K. D. Lemon, J. Carter, B. Hart, & C. Heisler (Eds.), *Domestic violence and children: Resolving custody disputes* (pp. 19–30). San Francisco: Family Violence Prevention Fund.

Jaffe, P. G., & Austin, G. (1995, July). *The impact of witnessing violence on children in custody and visitation disputes.* Paper presented at the Fourth International Family Violence Research Conference, Durham, NH.

Jaffe, P. G., & Geffner, R. (1998). Child custody disputes and domestic violence: Critical issues for mental health, social service, and legal professionals. In G. W. Holden, R. Geffner, & E. N. E. Jouriles (Eds.), *Children exposed to marital violence: Theory, research, and applied issues* (pp. 371–408). Washington, DC: American Psychological Association.

Jaffe, P. G., Lemon, N. K. D., Sandler, J., & Wolfe, D. A. (1996). *Working together to end domestic violence.* Tampa Bay, FL: Mancorp Publishing.

Jaffe, P. G., Poisson, S. E., & Cunningham, A. (2001). Domestic violence and high-conflict divorce: Developing a new generation of research for children. In S. A. Graham-Bermann & J. L. Edleson (Eds.), *Domestic violence in the lives of children* (pp. 189–202). Washington, DC: American Psychological Association.

Jaffe, P. G., Poisson, S. E., Cunningham, A., & Zerwer, M. (2001). *Access denied: The double disadvantage of poverty and domestic violence. An unpublished progress report submitted to the Atkinson Foundation.* London, ON: Authors.

Jaffe, P. G., Wolfe, D. A., & Wilson, S. K. (1990). *Children of battered women.* Thousand Oaks, CA: Sage.

Johnson, H., & Bunge, V. P. (2001). Prevalence and consequences of spousal assault in Canada. *Canadian Journal of Criminology, 43,* 27–45.

Johnston, J. R. (1994). High-conflict divorce. *Future of Children, 4,* 165–182.

Johnston, J. R., & Campbell, L. E. (1993). A clinical typology of interparental violence in disputed-custody divorces. *American Journal of Orthopsychiatry, 63,* 190–199.

Johnston, J. R., & Roseby, V. (1997). *In the name of the child: A developmental approach to understanding and helping children of conflicted and violent divorce.* New York: The Free Press.

Joint Committee on Domestic Violence. (1999). *Working toward a seamless community and justice response to domestic violence: A five year plan for Ontario (A report to the Attorney General of Ontario).* Toronto, ON: Author.

Jones, L., Hughes, M., & Unterstaller, U. (2001). Post-traumatic stress disorder (PTSD) in victims of domestic violence: A review of the research. *Trauma Violence and Abuse, 2,* 99–119.

Jouriles, E. N., McDonald, R., Norwood, W. D., & Ezell, E. (2001). Issues and controversies in documenting the prevalence of children's exposure to domestic violence. In S. A. Graham-Bermann & J. L. Edleson (Eds.), *Domestic violence in the lives ofchildren: The future of research, intervention and social policy* (pp. 13–34). Washington, DC: American Psychological Association.

Kane, R. J. (2000). Police responses to restraining orders in domestic violence incidents: Identifying the custody-threshold thesis. *Criminal Justice and Behavior, 27,* 561–580.

Kaye, M., & Tolmie, J. (1998). Fathers' rights groups in Australia and their engagement with issues in family law. *Australian Journal of Family Law, 12,* 19–31.

Kazarian, S. S., & Kazarian, L. Z. (1998). Cultural aspects of family violence. In S. S. Kazarian & D. R. Evans (Eds.), *Cultural clinical psychology: Theory, research, and practice* (pp. 316–347). New York: Oxford University Press.

Kerney McKenzie & Associates. (1998). *Review of the operation of Division 11 of the Family Law Reform Act to resolve inconsistencies between State family violence orders and contact orders made under family law.*

Kelly, J. B. (2000). Children's adjustment in conflicted marriage and divorce: A decade review of research. *Journal of the American Academy of Child and Adolescent Psychiatry, 39,* 963–973.

Kerig, P. K., Fedorowicz, A. E., Brown, C. A., Patenaude, R. L., & Warren, M. (1998). When warriors are worriers: Gender and children's coping with interpersonal violence. *Journal of Emotional Abuse, 1,* 89–114.

Kerr, G. S., & Jaffe, P. G. (1998, July). *Legal aspects of domestic violence and custody/access issues.* Paper presented at the National Family Law Program, Federation of Law Societies and Canadian Bar Association. Whistler, BC.

Kerr, G. S., & Jaffe, P. G. (1998). *Parental alienation syndrome and family law: A pragmatic perspective.* Paper presented at National Family Law Program, Federation of Law Societies and Canadian Bar Association. Whistler, BC.

Kerr, G. S., & Jaffe, P. G. (1998, July). *The clinical pitfalls in adopting the "parental alienation syndrome" in child custody disputes and "parental alienation syndrome" and family law: A pragmatic perspective.* Paper presented at the National Family Law Program, Federation of Law Societies and Canadian Bar Association. Whistler, BC.

Kerr, G. S., & Jaffe, P. G. (1999). Legal and clinical issues in child custody disputes involving domestic violence. *Canadian Family Law Quarterly,* 17, 1–37.

Kirn, W. (2000, September 25). Should you stay together for the kids? *Time.*

Leeder, E. (1988). Enmeshed in pain: Counseling the lesbian battering couple. *Women and Therapy, 7,* 81–99.

Lehmann, P. (1997). The development of posttraumatic stress disorder (PTSD) in a sample of child witnesses to mother assault. *Journal of Family Violence, 12,* 241-257.

Leighton, B. (1989). *Spousal abuse in Metropolitan Toronto: Research report on the response of the criminal justice system.* Ottawa, ON: Solicitor General Canada.

Lemon, N. K. D. (1990). *Domestic violence: What every judge should know.* San Francisco: California Center for Judicial Education and Research.

Lemon, N. K. D. (1995). *Domestic violence and children: Resolving custody and visitation disputes.* San Francisco, CA: Family Violence Prevention Fund.

Lemon, N. K. D., & Perry, A. (1996, June/July). Uniform Adoption Act considers domestic violence in placement and termination. *Domestic Violence Report, 1*(5), 1, 2, 15.

Lemon, N. K. D. (2000). Custody and visitation trends in the United States in domestic violence cases. In R. A. Geffner, P. G. Jaffe, & M. Suderman (Eds.), *Children exposed to family violence: Current issues in research, intervention, prevention, and policy development* (pp. 329–344). Binghamton, NY: Haworth Press.

Leonoff, A., & Montague, R. J. (1996). *Guide to custody and access assessments.* Toronto, ON, Canada: Carswell.

Levendosky, A. A., & Graham-Bermann, S. A. (2000). Behavioral observations of parenting in battered women. *Journal of Family Psychology, 14,* 80–94.

Levendosky, A. A., Huth-Bocks, A. C., Semel, M. A., & Shapiro, D. L. (2002). Trauma symptoms in preschool-age children exposed to domestic violence. *Journal of Interpersonal Violence, 17,* 150–164.

Levendosky, A. A., Lynch, S. M., & Graham-Bermann, S. A. (2000). Mothers' perceptions of the impact of woman abuse on their parenting. *Violence Against Women, 6,* 247–271.

Liss, M. B., & Stahly, G. B. (1993). Domestic violence and child custody. In M. Hansen & M. Haraway (Eds.), *Battering and family therapy: A feminist perspective* (pp. 175–187). Newbury Park, CA: Sage.

McAlister-Groves, B. (1999). Mental health services for children who witness domestic violence. *The Future of Children, 9,* 122–132.

McFarlane, J., Parker, B., Soeken, K., & Bullock, L. (1992). Assessing for abuse during pregnancy: Severity and frequency of injuries and associated entry into prenatal care. *Journal of the American Medical Association, 267,* 3176–3178.

McMahon, M., & Pence, E. (1995). Doing more harm than good? Some cautions on visitation centers. In E. Peled, P. G. Jaffe, & J. L. Edleson (Eds.), *Ending the cycle of violence: Community responses to children of battered women* (pp. 186–206). Thousand Oaks, CA: Sage.

Miami-Dade County Domestic Violence Fatality Review Team. (2000). *Aggregate data report.* Miami, FL: Author.

Moore, T. E., Pepler, D., Mae, R., & Michele, K. (1989). Effects of family violence on children: New directions for research and intervention. In B. Pressman & G. Cameron

(Eds.), *Intervening with assaulted women: Current theory, research, and practice* (pp. 75–91). Hillsdale, NJ: Lawrence Erlbaum Associates.

National Center for Health Statistics. (1998). Births, marriages, divorces and deaths: Provisional 1998 data. *National Vital Statistics Report, 47.*

National Council of Juvenile & Family Court Judges. (1994). *Model code on domestic and family violence* Reno, NV: Author.

National Council of Juvenile and Family Court Judges. (1990). *Family violence: Improving court practices.* Reno, NV: Author.

National Council of Juvenile and Family Court Judges. (1994). *Model code on domestic and family violence.* Reno, NV: Author.

National Council of Juvenile and Family Court Judges, Family Violence Project. (1995). Family violence in child custody statutes: An analysis of state codes and legal practice. *Family Law Quarterly, 29*(2), 197–227.

National Council of Juvenile and Family Court Judges. (1996). *Family violence legislative update.* Reno, NV: Author.

National Council of Juvenile and Family Court Judges. (1997). *Family violence legislative update.* Reno, NV: Author.

National Council of Juvenile and Family Court Judges. (1998). *Family violence legislative update.* Reno, NV: Author.

National Council of Juvenile and Family Court Judges. (1999). *Family violence legislative update.* Reno, NV: Author.

National Council of Juvenile and Family Court Judges. (2000). *A national judicial institute on domestic violence: Enhancing judicial skill in domestic violence cases.* Reno, NV: Author.

National Council of Juvenile and Family Court Judges. (2000). *Family violence legislative update.* Reno, NV: Author.

Newton, F. (2000). From the bench—Coconino County: Domestic violence—do judges really get it? *Family Law News, 1,* 1.

O'Sullivan, C. (2000). Estimating the population at risk for violence during child visitation. *Domestic Violence Report, 5,* 77–79.

Office of the Chief Coroner. (1998). *May/Iles Inquest.* Toronto, ON: Ministry of the Attorney General.

Office of the Chief Coroner. (2001). *Luft Inquest.* Toronto, ON: Ministry of the Attorney General.

Office of the Chief Coroner. (2002). *Hadley Inquest.* Toronto, ON: Ministry of the Attorney General.

Parkinson, P. (1995). Custody, access and domestic violence. *Australian Journal of Family Law, 9*(1), 41–57.

Peled, E., & Edleson, J. L. (1995). Process and outcome in small groups for children of battered women. In E. Peled, P. G. Jaffe, & J. L. Edleson (Eds.), *Ending the cycle of vio-*

lence: Community responses to children of battered women (pp. 77–96). Thousand Oaks, CA: Sage.

Perry, A. L., & Zorza, J. (2001). Can the "grave risk" exception to Hague convention cases protect children subject to family violence? *Domestic Violence Report, 6,* 17–18, 29–32.

Perry, B. D. (1995). Incubated in terror: Neurodevelopmental factors in the cycle of violence. In J. D. Osofsky (Ed.), *Children, youth and violence: Searching for solutions.* New York: Guilford Press.

Putt, J., & Higgins, K. (1997). *Violence against women in Australia.* Griffith ACT: Australian Institute of Criminology.

Quinsey, V. L., Harris, G. T., Rice, M. E., & Cormier, C. A. (1998). *Violent offenders: Appraising and managing risk.* Washington, DC: American Psychological Association.

Radford, L., & Hester, M. (2001). Overcoming mother blaming? Future directions for research on mothering and domestic violence. In S. A. Graham-Bermann & J. L. Edleson (Eds.), *Future directions for research on mothering and domestic violence* (pp. 135–155). Washington, DC: American Psychological Association.

Randolf, M., & Talamo, Y. (1997, June). *Multi-method evaluation of children who witness domestic violence.* Poster presented at the Second International Conference on Children Exposed to Domestic Violence, London, ON.

Reitzel, J. D., & Wolfe, D. A. (2001). Predictors of relationship abuse among young men. *Journal of Interpersonal Violence, 16,* 99–115.

Rennison, C. M., & Welchans, S. (2000). *Bureau of Justice Statistics special report: Intimate partner violence.* Washington, DC: U.S. Department of Justice.

Rhoades, H., Graycar, R., & Harrison, M. (1999). The Family Law Reform Act 1995: Can changing legislation change legal culture, legal practice and community expectations? University of Sydney [Online]. Available: www.law.usyd.edu.au/Research_Family_Court.html

Rodgers, K. (1994). *Wife assault: The findings of a national survey* (Rep. No. Juristat 14:9).

Rossman, B. B. R., Hughes, H. M., & Rosenberg, M. S. (2000). *Children and interparental violence: The impact of exposure.* Philadelphia: Brunner/Mazel.

Ruggiero, K. J., & McLeer, S. V. (2000). PTSD Scale of the Child Behavior Checklist: Concurrent and discriminant validity with non-clinic-referred sexually abused children. *Journal of Traumatic Stress, 13,* 287–299.

Schechter, S., & Edleson, J. L. (1998). *Effective intervention in domestic violence & child maltreatment cases: Guidelines for policy and practice.* Reno, NV: The National Council of Juvenile & Family Court Judges Family Violence Department.

Shaffer, M. (2001, February). *To grandmother's house we go? An examination of grandparent access.* Paper presented to The National Judical Institute Family Law Seminar, Halifax, NS.

Sheeran, M., & Hampton, S. (1999). Supervised visitation in cases of domestic violence. *Juvenile and Family Court Journal, 50,* 13–25.

Sherman, R. (1993, August 16). Gardner's law. *[US] National Law Journal,* p. 1.

Silvern, L., Karyl, J., & Landis, T. Y. (1995). Individual psychotherapy for the traumatized children of abused women. In E. Peled, P. G. Jaffe, & J. L. Edleson (Eds.), *Ending the cycle of violence: Community responses to children of battered women* (pp. 43–76). Thousand Oaks, CA: Sage.

Simonelli, C. J., Mullis, T., Elliott, A. N., & Pierce, T. W. (2002). Abuse by siblings and subsequent experiences of violence within the dating relationship. *Journal of Interpersonal Violence, 17,* 103–121.

Sinclair, D. (2000). *In the centre of the storm: 52 women speak out* (Durham region steering committee for custody and access issues affecting woman abuse survivors and their children) [Online]. Available: www.durhamresponsetowomanabuse.com

Singer, M. I., & Song, L. (1995). *Exposure to violence scales.* Cleveland, OH: Mandel School of Applied Social Sciences, Case Western Reserve University.

Smith, R., & Coukos, P. (1997, Fall). Fairness and accuracy in evaluations of domestic violence and child custody determinations. *Judges' Journal, 36*(4), 54–56.

Stahl, P. M. (1994). *Conducting child custody evaluations: A comprehensive guide.* Thousand Oaks, CA: Sage.

Statistics Canada. (2001). *Family violence in Canada: A statistical profile 2001.* Ottawa: Minister of Industry.

Statistics Canada: The Daily. (2000a). *Homicide statistics* (Rep. No. Wednesday, October 18, 2000).

Statistics Canada: The Daily. (2000b). *Major Releases.*

Sternberg, K. J., Lamb, M. E., Greenbaum, C., Cicchetti, D., Dawud, S., Cortes, R. M., Krispin, O., & Lorey, F. (1993). Effects of domestic violence on children's behavior problems and depression. *Developmental Psychology, 29,* 44–52.

Straus, M. A. (1979). Measuring intrafamily conflict and violence: The conflict tactics scale (CT) scales. *Journal of Marriage and the Family, 41,* 75–88.

Straus, M. A. (1992). Children as witnesses to marital violence: A risk factor for lifelong problems among a nationally representative sample of American men and women. In D. F. Schwarz (Ed.), *Children and violence: Report on the 23rd Ross Roundtable on critical approaches to common pediatric problems* (pp. 98–104). Columbus, OH: Ross Laboratories.

Straus, M. A., Gelles, R. J., & Steinmetz, S. K. (1980). *Behind closed doors: Violence in the American family.* Garden City, NY: Anchor Books.

Straus, M. A., Hamby, S. L., Boney-McCoy, S., & Sugarman, D. B. (1996). The revised Conflict Tactics Scales (CTS2): Development and preliminary psychometric data. *Journal of Family Issues, 17,* 283–316.

Sudermann, M., & Jaffe, P. G. (1999). *A handbook for health and social service providers and educators on children exposed to woman abuse/family violence.* Ottawa, ON: Minister of Public Works and Government Services Canada.

Sullivan, C. M., Nguyen, H., Allen, N., Bybee, D., & Juras, J. (2000). Beyond searching for deficits: Evidence that physically and emotionally abused women are nurturing parents. *Journal of Emotional Abuse, 2,* 51–71.

Sullivan, C. M., Juras, J., & Bybee, D. (2000). How children's adjustment is affected by their relationships to their mothers' abusers. *Journal of Interpersonal Violence, 15,* 587–602.

Supervised Access Program Ministry of the Attorney General. (2000). *Best practice manual for supervised access service providers.* Toronto, ON: Author.

Susser, K. (2001). Recognizing domestic violence in family law proceedings. *Fordham Urban Law Journal, 27,* 190–242.

The London Coordinating Committee to End Woman Abuse. (2001). *A 20 year review of achievement.* London, ON: Author.

Tjaden, P., & Thoennes, N. (2000). *Full report of the prevalence, incidence, and consequences of violence against women: Findings from the national violence against women survey.* Washington, DC: U.S. Department of Justice, Office of Justice Programs.

Turkat, I. D. (1997, Spring). Parental alienation syndrome: Management of visitation interference. *Judges' Journal, 36*(2), 17–21, 47.

Underwood, N. (2002, January 21). The happy divorce. *McLean's,* 7–10.

Walker, L. E. (1979). *The battered woman.* New York: Harper & Row.

Wallerstein, J. S., & Blakeslee, S. (1989). *Second chances: Men, women, and children a decade after divorce.* New York: Ticknor and Fields.

Wallerstein, J. S., Lewis, J. M., & Blakeslee, S. (2000). *The unexpected legacy of divorce: A 25-year landmark study.* New York: Hyperion.

Websdale, N., Town, M., & Johnson, B. (1999). Domestic violence fatality reviews: From a culture of blame to a culture of safety. *Juvenile and Family Court Journal, 50,* 61–74.

Weiner, M. H. (2000). International child abduction and the escape from domestic violence. *Fordham L.aw Review, 69,* 593–706.

Weissman, D. M. (2001). Gender-based violence as judicial anomaly: Between "the truly national and truly local." *Boston College Law Review, 42,* 1081–1159.

Weisz, A. N., Tolman, R. M., & Saunders, D. G. (2000). Assessing the risk of severe domestic violence: The importance of survivors' predictions. *Journal of Interpersonal Violence, 15,* 75–90.

Weithorn, L. A. (2001). Protecting children from exposure to domestic violence: The use and abuse of child maltreatment status. *Hastings Law Journal, 53,* 1–156.

Woffordt, S., Mihalic, D. E., & Menard, S. (1994). Continuities in marital violence. *Journal of Family Violence, 9,* 195–225.

Wolfe, D. A., & Jaffe, P. G. (1999). Emerging strategies in the prevention of domestic violence. *The Future of Children, 9,* 133–144.

Wolfe, V. V., Gentile, C., Michienzi, T., Sas, L., & Wolfe, D. A. (1991). The Children's Impact of Traumatic Events Scale: A measure of post-sexual abuse PTSD symptoms. *Behavioral Assessment, 13,* 359–383.

Wood, C. L. (1994). The parental alienation syndrome: A dangerous aura of reliability. *Loyola of Los Angeles Law Review, 27,* 1367–1415.

Zorza, J. (1995). How abused women can use the law to help protect their children. In E. Peled, P. G. Jaffe, & J. L. Edleson (Eds.), *Ending the cycle of violence: Community responses to children of battered women* (pp. 147–169). Thousand Oaks, CA: Sage.

Zorza, J. (1997). Domestic violence seldom considered in psychologists' child custody recommendations. *Domestic Violence Report, 2,* 65–80.

Zorza, J. (1999, October/November). The UCCJEA: Why do we have it and how does it help battered women in custody disputes? *Domestic Violence Report, 1,* 11–16.

Index

About the Authors

Peter G. Jaffe, Ph.D., is the Founding Director (1975–2001) and Special Advisor on Violence Prevention of the Centre for Children and Families in the Justice System of the London Family Court Clinic. He is also a member of the Clinical Adjunct Faculty for the Departments of Psychology and Psychiatry at the University of Western Ontario, former chair of the Board of Directors of the Battered Women's Advocacy Centre, and past Chairperson and a founding board member of the Board of Directors for the Centre for Research on Violence Against Women and Children. He gives presentations on domestic violence and violence prevention to teachers, students, lawyers, judges, police, doctors, clergy, and various community groups. He has collaborated with the Family Violence Department of the National Council of Juvenile and Family Court Judges and the Family Violence Prevention Fund in developing innovative training programs on domestic violence for judges across the United States. He is the recipient of many awards and grants, author of numerous research articles, and coauthor of four books on the subject of children exposed to domestic violence, including the landmark publication *Children of Battered Women* (coauthored by D. Wolfe and S. Wilson and published by Sage in 1990).

Nancy K. D. Lemon, J.D., is a consultant to the California Center for Judicial Education and Research (CJER), with whom she developed curricula for new judges and for court employees. As an undergraduate, she helped create the first University of California Women's Studies major and received a B.A. with honors from the University of California at Santa Cruz in 1975. Following her graduation from Boalt Hall School of Law (University of California at Berkeley) in 1980, she specialized in domestic violence legal issues. Since 1988, she has taught Domestic Violence Law at Boalt, where she wrote *Domestic Violence Law,* the first published curriculum on this topic, published in 1996 and

2001. While working at various nonprofit agencies around the San Francisco Bay Area from 1981 through 1993, she represented hundreds of battered women, obtaining restraining orders and advocating for them within the civil and criminal justice systems. She has been active with the Policy and Research Committee of the California Alliance Against Domestic Violence since 1984 and has consulted on numerous pieces of legislation. She is the Associate Editor of *Domestic Violence Report*, a U.S. bimonthly national publication, and has published many books and articles in this field. She has worked with other attorneys as a trial consultant and has testified as an expert witness on domestic violence issues.

Samantha E. Poisson, M.Ed., is Clinical/Research Services Coordinator at the Centre for Children and Families in the Justice System of the London Family Court Clinic and is currently completing her doctorate in education in applied psychology at the University of Toronto. She has published articles and chapters on family violence, research, and custody and access issues, including "Domestic Violence and High-Conflict Divorce: Developing a New Generation of Research for Children" in the book *Domestic Violence in the Lives of Children*, edited by S. Graham-Berman and J. Edleson. Her teaching experience has involved presentations and workshops involving prosecutors, family lawyers, social workers, and advocates for abused women and children. As well as her active involvement in research and training, she has worked extensively in the area of child-custody assessments and provided expert testimony in Ontario, New Brunswick, and Saskatchewan.